Developing Computer-Based Library Systems

Developing Computer-Based Library Systems

by John Corbin

A Neal-Schuman Professional Book

ORYX PRESS
1981

The rare Arabian Oryx is believed to have inspired the myth of the unicorn. This desert antelope became virtually extinct in the early 1960s. At that time several groups of international conservationists arranged to have 9 animals sent to the Phoenix Zoo to be the nucleus of a captive breeding herd. Today the Oryx population is nearing 300 and herds have been returned to reserves in Israel, Jordan, and Oman.

Library of Congress Cataloging in Publication Data

Corbin, John Boyd.
    Developing computer-based library systems.

    (A Neal-Schuman professional book)
    Bibliography: p.
    Includes index.
    1. Libraries—Automation. 2. Information storage and retrieval systems. I. Title.
Z678.9.C63   025.3'028'54   81-1232
ISBN 0-912700-10-6   AACR2

Contents

Chapter 5. Detailed Design Specifications   59

The Modular Approach
Input and Output Specifications
Processing Specifications
Data Base Specifications
Other Design Specifications
Design Documentation

Chapter 6. Acquisition of Hardware, Software, and Vendor Assistance   73

RFP Development
Decision Rules for Selecting the Best Response
Solicitation of Responses to an RFP
Validation of Responses from Vendors
Contract Negotiation

Chapter 7. System Implementation   88

Space Layout
Site Preparation
Job Descriptions
Staff Orientation and Training
Library Patron Orientation
Acquisitions of Special Supplies, Equipment, and Forms
File Creation
Installation and Check of Hardware and Software
System Activation
System Evaluation and Acceptance

Appendices

Preface

Relatively few libraries had hope or desire of using computers prior to the 1970s. During the past few years, however, growing demands for new and sophisticated approaches to information access and dissemination, an inability to cope with an expanding and increasingly complex information base, rising costs, and insufficient funding have forced librarians to seek better and more cost-efficient systems for providing services. The use of computer-based systems potentially could alleviate some of these pressures. Computers now are commonplace in most institutions and organizations where libraries exist or in networks serving libraries; hence, most libraries have ready access to computing power. Indeed, technological advances and competition within the computer industry have reduced the size and cost of hardware to the point that many libraries can afford to have their own in-house computers dedicated solely to library use.

A computer-based library system is developed and integrated into the library organization in an effort referred to as a *systems project,* and librarians with the necessary skills to plan, design, and implement systems in such an undertaking are in great demand. In most small or not-so-wealthy libraries, however, no one has the training and experience required to perform the exacting, time-consuming, yet absolutely vital job of laying an adequate groundwork for these radically new, complex systems. The purpose of this book is to provide a practical handbook and guide for the librarian untrained in systems development and perhaps unfamiliar with computers, but nonetheless responsible for developing a computer-based system. The emphasis is upon the planning, organization, management, and step-by-step processes of a systems project.

The text of the book is organized into seven chapters. Chapter 1 presents an overview of the systems approach, elements of computer-based library systems, methods of developing computer-based systems, and advantages and disadvantages of using the systems. Chapter 2 outlines the activities essential for project initiation and management, with an emphasis upon planning and staffing. Chapter 3 describes the process of defining the library's requirements for the new system to be developed, an important preliminary activity in any project. Chapter 4 presents a methodology for evaluating and comparing alternative systems and selecting the best for development. Chapter 5 is devoted to the development of detailed design specifications necessary when a system must be developed from scratch locally. Chapter 6 is concerned with the acquisition of any hardware, software, hardware and software maintenance, and/or other vendor assistance essential to install and support a system under development. Emphasis in this chapter is upon the preparation of a request for proposal (RFP) and the evaluation of responses from vendors to this document. Chapter 7 outlines the activities essential during system implementation, including site preparation, staff training and orientation, file conversion, acquisition of special supplies, equipment, and forms, and new system activation, evaluation, and acceptance.

A detailed list of phases, activities, and steps for a typical project to develop a computer-based system is given in the appendices, in addition to examples of the documents which are generated during a project. A glossary contains definitions of terms included in the book, and a bibliography of allied readings which might be helpful to the beginning project manager is included.

Developing Computer-Based Library Systems

Chapter 1
Introduction

The purpose of this introductory chapter is to provide some general background information for a project to develop a computer-based library system. Specifically, it includes overviews and descriptions of:

- The systems approach.
- Elements of computer-based library systems.
- Methods of developing computer-based library systems.
- Advantages and disadvantages of using computer-based systems.

THE SYSTEMS APPROACH

A library is composed of a number of separate but interrelated and interacting parts called *systems,* arranged in a hierarchical network according to size and importance.

Definition of a Library System. A library system is an organized set of activities, tasks, or operations performed on information, library materials, or other physical objects to achieve a specified end result or purpose. Examples of large systems in a library include acquisitions, cataloging, circulation, and reference or information systems.

Definition of a Computer-Based Library System. In a traditional or manual library system humans perform the required processing operations, but if a computer is used to perform some or all of the work a *computer-based library system* results. In such a system, humans and the computer usually share responsibility for performing the work. For example, a human might perform the first 5 processing operations; a computer, the next 100 operations; a human, the next 20 operations; and so on.

Due to this sharing of responsibilities, today's computer-based library systems actually should be referred to as "human-machine systems," or, literally, "systems in which humans are assisted by a computer." The computer is merely a tool (albeit a marvelous one) enabling librarians to do something less expensively, more accurately, or more rapidly than by manual methods. Completely automated or automatic library systems, in which no human intervention and control are necessary, do not exist and are not likely until the end of the century and beyond.

The Systems Hierarchy. Each large system in the library can consist of a number of smaller systems called *subsystems*. A circulation system, for example, might contain component borrower registration, checkout, check-in, and overdues systems (Figure 1-1). The result of this division is another level of systems, some of which might be divided still further into even smaller subsystems. For example, the checkout system might consist of regular, reserve, and special checkout subsystems. The process of dividing a large system into smaller and smaller subsystems can continue as long as is practical or possible.

Figure 1-1. The hierarchical levels of systems of a library.

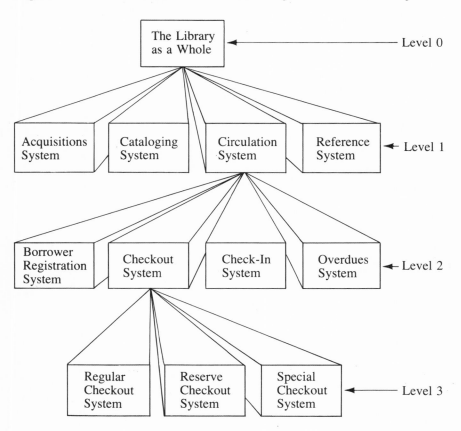

Thus, a network of "systems within systems" exists throughout the library, organized into hierarchical levels conforming usually but not always to traditional organization chart lines, and ranging from very large and general systems at the top of the hierarchy to very small and specific systems at the bottom. While each system or subsystem is functionally independent of all others, no system on any level can exist by itself or in isolation from other systems.

ELEMENTS OF COMPUTER-BASED LIBRARY SYSTEMS

Each computer-based library system is composed of a number of elements. Each system:

1. Has one or more *goals* or *purposes*.
2. Requires an *input* of information, materials, or other physical objects.
3. Performs specified *processing operations* on the input.
4. Produces end results called *output*.
5. Requires an *environment* in which to exist.
6. Requires computing, software, data communications, human, information, and other miscellaneous *resources* in order to operate.

A schematic model depicting these elements is shown in Figure 1-2.

Figure 1-2. A schematic model depicting the elements of a computer-based library system.

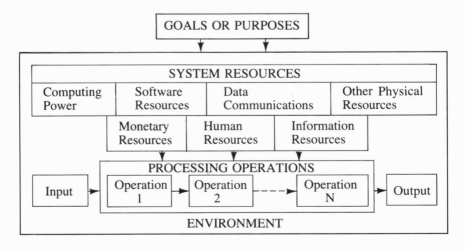

System Goals or Purposes. A library system has one or more goals or purposes which state the mission or achievements toward which efforts in maintaining and operating the system are directed. For example, the goals of a circulation system might be to loan informational materials to legitimate borrowers in good standing and provide accountability for the successful return of the loans, and of an acquisitions system to acquire informational materials efficiently for a library's collections through purchases, gifts, and exchanges and provide a reliable means of controlling and reporting the expenditure of acquisitions funds. System goals are long-range and usually not subject to change over the years.

System Input. Each system requires an input of information, library materials, or other physical objects as raw material to be converted or processed into a desired output. Most library systems require an input of a combination of information and physical objects.

Because library work is oriented around and dependent upon information, most library systems require either verbal or recorded information as the primary or only input. Information as system input includes the following:

1. *Textual information* forms the contents of books, pamphlets, journals, films, filmstrips, videotapes, and other materials which constitute a library's holdings.
2. *Bibliographic and citation information* describes materials for cataloging, indexing, and location purposes, and forms the basis of a library's catalogs and indexes to its collections and of general bibliographies and indexes providing access to recorded knowledge both inside and outside the library.
3. *Abstract information* is an abridgement or summary giving the essential points of books, articles, and other materials.
4. *Transaction information* is contained in the thousands of circulation transaction cards, reference or information requests, interlibrary loan requests, selection slips, invoices and vouchers, overdue and fines notices, memoranda between staff, and other transactions that are generated in a library's acquisitions, fund accounting, cataloging, circulation, information services, administrative, and other systems.
5. *Management information* is contained in the plans, budgets, work reports, annual reports, statistics, personnel records, and inventory records which are used in controlling and managing the library as an organization.

Some systems also require an input of physical materials such as books, journals, microforms, and other materials or objects such as borrower cards and currency, although usually a system is concerned with the *information* contained in or represented by these things rather than with the objects themselves. An acquisitions system, for example, might require an input of bibliographic and transaction information recorded in advertisements, selection slips, order cards, or pages from reviewing journals. In addition to recorded information, other systems might require an input of books, journals, microforms, films, filmstrips, videotapes, and other items which will be processed in some manner to produce the desired output. A cataloging system, for example, might require an input of both materials to be processed and bibliographic and transaction information recorded on processing slips or cards.

System Processing Operations. Every library system has a set or group of specified processing operations which are performed on the input of information, library materials, or other physical objects. The system input is converted to output as these step-by-step tasks are performed. Common information processing operations include:

1. *Origination*—the capturing or recording of information through handwriting, keyboarding, or other means as events or transactions occur.
2. *Verification*—the checking or validation of captured information to ensure that it is correct before processing continues.
3. *Classification*—the systematic grouping of information into classes such as type of transaction, material, or borrower.
4. *Sorting*—arranging information into a predetermined order or sequence or selecting particular information from a larger mass.
5. *Calculation*—the arithmetic manipulation of information through addition, subtraction, multiplication, division, or logical comparisons required in such applications as funds accounting, purchase order preparation, fines calculation, and statistics compilation.
6. *Storage*—the placement of information into a file.
7. *Retrieval*—the searching, selection, and removal of specific information from a file.
8. *Summarization*—the reduction or compression of a mass of information into a more concise or meaningful form.
9. *Reproduction*—the duplication of information from one medium to another or the production of one or more copies of information.
10. *Dissemination*—the communication, transfer, or movement of information from one location to another by verbal, physical, or electronic means.

Common physical operations required to handle or process materials and other items include moving, inserting, sorting, storing, retrieving, pasting, opening, closing, gathering, cutting, lifting, removing, turning, and many others. Although paper, film, magnetic tape, plastic badges, and other physical materials and objects may be required to record, store, and transport information, library systems usually are concerned only with the information contained in or represented by these media rather than with the materials themselves; the physical media are merely *containers* of desired information.

Information processing and physical operations are used repeatedly in a computer-based library system in selecting, acquiring, cataloging, classifying, processing, storing, locating, retrieving, and disseminating information and materials to users. In many library systems, the processing of information parallels that of processing materials and other physical objects. Each task or operation, performed in an orderly sequence, is necessary to convert the system input into the desired output. The movement of information and materials and other items from operation to operation through a system is referred to as *work flow*.

System Output. Each computer-based library system produces end results called *output*, which is processed input. Examples of system output include materials acquired and physically processed; records and reports prepared; lists and bibliographies produced; interlibrary loan transactions completed; and other products or results achieved by performing prescribed operations on input. Often, the output of one system later becomes the input to another system. For example, the output of an acquisitions system (materials acquired) becomes input (materials to be cataloged, classified, and otherwise processed) into a cataloging system. The output of a system also can be stated as a conditional change in information or materials. For example, output can be verified information (that is, unverified information is processed into verified information) and labeled materials (that is, unlabeled materials are processed into labeled materials).

System Environment. A system must be housed and operated in a finite amount of physical space, with proper levels of lighting, temperature, humidity, noise control, and cleanliness. It should be noted that several systems which use some or all of the same resources can occupy the same physical space.

Computing Power. An indispensable resource for a computer-based library system is computing power, furnished by a digital computer. The machine supplying this resource may be located in the library, in a data processing center or service bureau serving the library's host institution, or in a local or distant networking organization.

A computer is an electronic device which accepts and automatically performs prescribed and organized sequences of processing operations on information to achieve a desired end result or purpose. The type of computer of interest to libraries, the general-purpose digital computer, operates on information represented as symbols in discrete form as opposed to information in the form of continuously changing physical variables such as electrical current, voltage, pressure, or temperature. Such a computer, which is designed to solve a broad class of problems in almost any discipline or field including that of librarianship or information science, can be used to control processes, store and retrieve information, maintain files of information, perform computations upon data, and arrange and rearrange data.

Many sizes of digital computers, with varying capabilities and sophistication, are available. Several arbitrary size classes are used today. The librarian is warned, however, that the categories are not precisely defined and can be misleading. Also, size now bears little relationship to a computer's ability to perform well; some small computers are capable of performing as well as, and sometimes better than, other larger machines. Modern computers are classed into 4 loosely defined categories:

1. *Microcomputer*. The microcomputer is the smallest class or size of computer today. It is a small, programmable device, as small as a pocket calculator or as large as a home stereo receiver, useful in a wide range of home, business, and industrial applications and usually designed to handle a restricted number of applications or, in some cases, only one application. The microcomputer often is used as an integral part of larger computer systems, for example, to control communications from a number of terminal devices into a larger computer or as part of the terminal itself to perform some preprocessing functions such as information editing and error detection before data are transmitted to a larger machine.

2. *Minicomputer*. The minicomputer also is a small, programmable device which is fast and reliable and useful in a wide range of business, industrial, and library applications. Many libraries now have in-house minicomputers dedicated to their sole use. The machine might be the size of a home stereo receiver or a portable typewriter and fit on a desk, although some minis are housed in floor-standing cabinets along with other essential equipment. Some minicomputers can handle only one application at a time, but most can handle several sets of instructions and users simultaneously. Some are used independently of other computer sys-

tems, while others are connected to larger systems and dependent upon them for mass storage and some processing.

3. *Medium-Sized Computer.* Between the minicomputer and the large-scale computer is the medium-sized machine, sometimes referred to as the *midicomputer*. This size computer is fast and versatile and can handle many applications and users at the same time. It is most often found in a data processing or computer center serving a number of different users, but some large libraries have this size machine in-house solely for their use. A medium-sized computer without auxiliary equipment might be the size of an office copier or larger. As little as 400 or more than 1,000 square feet of physical floor space might be required to house and maintain this type of computer, depending upon the peripheral equipment.

4. *Large-Scale Computer.* A large-scale computer is the largest, fastest, and most versatile type of computer, with large amounts of mass storage, a wide range of auxiliary equipment, and an ability to handle many applications and users at the same time. Only large organizations or a data processing or computer center serving many users need or can afford this type of computer, which might require thousands of square feet of floor space.

The metallic, plastic, magnetic, electric, electronic, and other physical parts of a computer are referred to as *hardware*. Regardless of its size, capabilities, or cost, a computer system is usually composed of 4 basic hardware elements (Figure 1-3):

1. *Central Processing Unit.* The computer proper is referred to as the *central processing unit* (CPU) or *central processor* and consists of primary storage, control, and arithmetic-logic units. In large machines, the primary storage unit may be a separate unit unto itself. The purpose of the primary storage unit is to hold information being processed and step-by-step instructions for processing that information. The control unit interprets instructions for processing data and directs and coordinates the computer in executing these instructions. The arithmetic-logic unit contains the circuitry for adding, subtracting, dividing, and comparing information according to the sets of instructions or programs.

2. *Auxiliary Storage.* Auxiliary storage supplements the primary storage unit of a computer and provides a mass storage capability to the system. Common auxiliary storage devices include magnetic disk, magnetic tape, and sometimes magnetic drum, which can

store larger amounts of information than can primary storage. When information in an auxiliary storage device is to be processed by the computer, it must be routed through primary storage. Each auxiliary storage device is connected by electrical cable to, and is under direct control of, the central processing unit.

3. *Input Devices*. Input devices provide a means by which information can be entered into the computer for processing. Common methods of input include a typewriterlike keyboard, punched cards, paper tape, magnetic tape, optical characters, and bar codes. Each method requires its own special device connected by electrical cable to and under direct control of the central processing unit.

4. *Output Devices*. The results of processing can be output on a cathode ray tube (CRT) or visual display screen, printed on paper, punched in cards or paper tape, or encoded on magnetic tape or magnetic disk. Each method also requires its own special device connected by electrical cable to and under direct control of the central processing unit. It is common for input and output devices to be contained in the same piece of equipment.

Figure 1-3. A schematic model of the elements of a computer system.

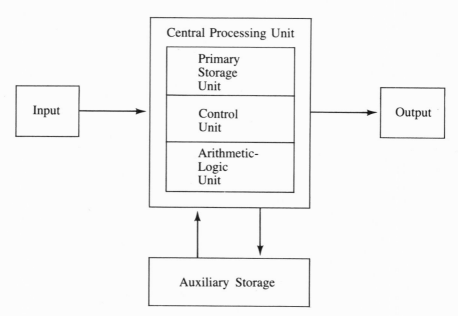

Computer Software. Another important resource in a computer-based library system is computer software. Software refers to the collection of computer instructions or programs necessary to drive a computer system. Computer hardware can not operate without software, which is of 2 basic types:

- *Application software* refers to the sets of computer instructions or programs required for specific applications such as library acquisitions, cataloging, circulation, or reference. A different set of instructions is required for each application or job the computer is to perform; in most complex systems, many sets might be necessary for a particular application. This type of software must be purchased or leased from a software vendor, shared with other libraries, borrowed and adapted from other libraries, or designed and prepared locally. The programs can be written in a variety of programming languages such as COBOL, FORTRAN, PL/1, and BASIC and contained or stored in punched cards or on magnetic tape or magnetic disk.
- *System software,* which usually is supplied by the hardware manufacturer, is necessary to maintain and operate a computer system and to facilitate the programming, testing, debugging, and running of application software. Examples of system software include, among others, operating systems, programming language systems, utility programs, and data base management systems.

Software also can include operating manuals and guides, circuit diagrams, technical manuals, and other documentation associated with computer hardware and the application and system software.

Data Communications. A resource which might be required by a computer-based library system is some type of data communications system. Data communications is the transmission or transfer of information and messages from one point, person, or equipment to another over communications links or channels.

In the early days of computing, all information to be processed for a library had to be taken in batches to a central computing center, the work placed in a queue, and the results trundled back to the library after the input was processed. While this method still is effective and economical, technological advances and a convergence of computer with communications technologies make this tedious process unnecessary. In a modern online computer system, information and instructions can be entered into a terminal device located in the library, then transmitted to a remote computer via cables or other communications links such as ordinary telephone lines. After processing the information, the computer returns the results to the library over the same links. Thus, computing power can be brought into the library at any point where it is needed—at the circulation desk, the reference center, or the technical services work station—and where communications links can be installed.

The data communications process normally is bidirectional: that is, information can be transmitted from the library to a remote computer for processing, then back to the library, using the same equipment and channels. Output returned to the library from the remote computer is accepted by a receiving terminal. Usually, transmitting and receiving are performed in the same terminal device. However, if one method is desired for input and another for output, then different types of terminals are required. For example, information can be entered into the data communications system via a paper tape reader, but the results of the computer's processing can be returned for output on a printer.

There are 5 basic steps in the data communication process, as shown in Figure 1-4:

1. *Information Input.* Input into a data communications system is accomplished by entering information to be transmitted from the library to a remote computer for processing into a transmitting device such as the keyboard of a CRT or typewriter terminal or a punched card, paper tape, or magnetic tape reader. The terminal device converts the input entered into a stream of digital pulses of electricity representing the characters of information.

2. *Signal Modulation.* The information converted into electrical signals by the transmitting terminal is in a digital form which must be converted or modified to a form acceptable to the channel over which it is to be transmitted. A device called a *modem* (*mo*dulator-*dem*odulator) is used to convert the signals for transmission. A variety of modems is available for use in the library.

3. *Information Transmission.* Information is transmitted from the library to the remote computer over communications links or channels. Common communications channels include telegraph and telephone lines, radio links, coaxial cables, microwave, and satellite. If the distance between the library and the computer is short, information can be transmitted successfully over cables strung between the 2 points, but signals to be sent further than several hundred feet can become so distorted that the information content is lost. For longer distances, most libraries use the facilities of a *common carrier*, which is a public utility company recognized by an appropriate regulatory agency such as the Feder-

al Communications Commission as having a vested interest in and responsibility for furnishing communications services to the general public. Examples of communications common carriers include the American Telephone and Telegraph Company (AT&T), General Telephone (GTE), Western Union, Tymshare, and others.

These carriers offer 2 common types of links or channels. *Dial-up* or *public-switched lines* are commonly used for data communication. These channels require that a connection be made through an operator or an automatic switching center. The ordinary telephone line is the best example of a dial-up facility. The link is available as long as a connection is made; payment varies according to mileage, time of the day or night, and duration of the connect time. The great advantage of using this type of link is that telephones are everywhere, and wherever one is located a data communications system can be established. However, the carrier does not guarantee the quality of transmission over this type of line. *Private* or *leased lines,* the second type of channel, remain connected for the duration of a lease, and the leasee has unlimited use of the facility. These lines can be conditioned by adding special equipment to maintain a quality of transmission with a certain standard of permissible error rate.

There are 3 basic modes of transmitting information over data communications lines. A *simplex* channel can transmit only in one direction. This type is used, for example, for a remote device which can receive but not transmit. A *half-duplex* channel can transmit in both directions but in only one direction at a time. A *full-duplex* channel can transmit in both directions at the same time, using 2 channels. One channel is equipped for transmission in one direction, and the other in the opposite direction.

The grade of a channel indicates its capacity to transmit information, usually measured in terms of *bandwidth*. Bandwidth refers to the range of frequencies within which a channel can transmit, measured in *cycles per second* (cps) or *hertz*. However, the ability of a channel to transmit information usually is measured in terms of *bits per second* (bps), which is roughly the equivalent to the *baud rate*. Low-speed or narrow-band channels, which were originally developed for teletypewriters, are the narrowest or the lowest-grade channel, capable of transmitting data up to 300 bps. Medium-speed or voice-band channels are used both for human voice and data communications. Typical transmission speed is from 300 to 9600 bps. High-speed, broadband, or wideband channels are used for communication requiring high data transfer rates. They are usually composed of groups of voice-grade channels which can carry voice, computer data, or facsimile signals. Over 50,000 bps can be transmitted over switched channels and up to 250,000 bps over private-line channels.

4. *Signal Demodulation.* At the other end of the communications channel or link, the signals transmitted must be converted or modified back to digital form by another modem before the computer can accept and process the information.

5. *Information Output.* Information as output in the data communications system is received by the computer itself or another device. When a computer system has a large number of remote terminals using its central processing unit, a device called a *communications processor* may be used. Such a device, which itself is a type of computer, can handle incoming and outgoing messages, message queues and priorities, error checking, routing messages into the central processing unit, and other similar tasks. The central processing unit then is relieved of these functions.

Figure 1-4. A schematic model of a data communications system.

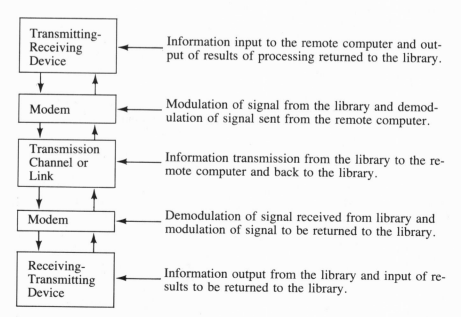

Transmitting-Receiving Device	Information input to the remote computer and output of results of processing returned to the library.
Modem	Modulation of signal from the library and demodulation of signal sent from the remote computer.
Transmission Channel or Link	Information transmission from the library to the remote computer and back to the library.
Modem	Demodulation of signal received from library and modulation of signal to be returned to the library.
Receiving-Transmitting Device	Information output from the library and input of results to be returned to the library.

Several other devices can be used to control or regulate the communications traffic to and from a computer. A *transmission control unit* or *line controller* enables the computer to monitor and control the flow of information from remote terminals into the system for processing, then back to the remote locations. Each line into the computer through this device is called a *port*. A *multiplexer* is a device which accepts input from several terminals, combines their signals, then transmits them together, simultaneously, over one communications channel. A similar unit at the other end of the transmission link separates the signals before entry into the computer for processing. Multiplexing enables a number of low-speed or low-activity terminals to have economical access to a central processing unit by sharing a single communications channel. A *concentrator* is similar to a multiplexer, but allows only one terminal or the central processing unit connected to it to use an available channel at any one time. The device queries or polls each terminal and the CPU one after another; whenever a channel is idle, the first ready to send a message is given control of the link. A channel in use by one terminal or by the CPU is unavailable to all others.

Other Physical Resources. The computer system and data communications facilities used within a computer-based library system are considered physical resources. Other physical resources which may be required by a system as it operates include consumable supplies such as forms, pencils, ink, paper clips, typewriter and printer ribbons, and electrical energy, and nonconsumable equipment such as desks, chairs, filing cabinets, shelving, typewriters, and other machines and devices.

Human Resources. Human resources and energy are required to perform system operations, provide management and planning for a system, and service machines and equipment used by a system.

Monetary Resources. Monetary resources are required to buy the physical and human resources necessary to maintain and operate a system. Since any system must operate within the limits of a budget imposed upon it, the availability of funds dictates the amount of other resources available to operate a system and, therefore, limits the type, quality, and quantity of output.

Information Resources. Each computer-based library system requires a store of information which can be used as necessary for input or output. The largest information resource available to library systems is that stored in books, pamphlets, journals, documents, reports, films, filmstrips, videotapes, and other materials. Bibliographic, citation, and abstracting indexes and catalogs also can be considered resources if they are used as a source of input into a system. Other databases and files used as a resource by systems include borrower, in-process, vendor, and fund accounting files, among others.

METHODS OF DEVELOPING COMPUTER-BASED LIBRARY SYSTEMS

A library could have one or more of several types of computer-based systems operating simultaneously in its organization. These systems can best be characterized by the methods by which they were developed. There are 4 basic methods by which libraries develop computer-based systems:

- Purchasing or leasing a turnkey system.

- Sharing a system with other libraries through networking.

- Adapting the system of another library for local use.

- Developing a system locally from scratch.

Purchasing or Leasing Turnkey Systems. A turnkey system is one which has been designed, programmed and tested, then offered for sale or lease by a company to libraries, ready to be installed and operated. Most turnkey systems are for the circulation function, but some are for acquisitions and other library applications.

These packaged or off-the-shelf systems typically include a mini-computer and all other essential hardware, system software, application software, and necessary documentation such as operating and procedure manuals. Some turnkey system vendors contract to install and maintain both hardware and software and train the library staff to operate and manage the system. Other turnkey vendors offer the application software only, and the library is responsible for providing the necessary hardware and system software for its support.

Developing a computer-based system by acquiring and installing a turnkey system has several advantages:

1. Usually, a turnkey system can be installed in the library within a few months or less.

2. The costly and time-consuming design, programming, and testing of a system by the library can be eliminated because the vendor has already spent the months or possibly years which must be devoted to these important activities.

3. Thus, the library need not have access to computer and systems specialists, because this expertise also is provided by the turnkey system vendor.

4. While the library staff must learn to operate and manage the turnkey system, usually no special computer background is a prerequisite.

Some disadvantages of acquiring and installing a turnkey system include:

1. It is costly. The library purchasing or leasing a turnkey system is paying a portion of the vendor's development and marketing costs in addition to the firm's expected profit. However, although it might at first glance appear expensive, this type of system probably does not cost more than any other if all developmental costs are considered in the comparison.

2. A turnkey system may have been designed for average or typical libraries. Therefore, it might have undesirable features which must be accepted by the library or might lack desirable features, thus forcing the library to compromise its individual needs to the packaged systems. However, many of the newer and more successful turnkey systems are flexible and can be tailored easily to satisfy most library requirements.

3. Some turnkey systems are inflexible and can not be altered, once installed, to meet changing needs and conditions within the library without extensive and costly overhauls.

4. The computer must be housed in a nonpublic area where electrical power, heating and air conditioning, noise, and dust can be controlled.

Sharing Systems through Networking. A system shared through networking is one which has been designed, programmed, and tested by a networking organization or a commercial firm, then offered for use by many libraries on a shared basis. The network may be operated by non-profit organizations such as OCLC, Inc. (formerly the Ohio College Library Center) or by commercial firms such as Baker and Taylor, Brodart, and others. A library can contract with the network or other organization for services such as shared cataloging, file conversion, bibliographic verification, acquisitions, interlibrary loans, serials control, online reference services, and others made available for use by many libraries. Payment for use of a system could be through membership dues and/or service and transaction fees.

Typically, one or more computer terminals in a participating library are connected into a data communications system to a computer located in the same city, the next state, or thousands of miles away. Each library can have its own communications link or share a common channel with others directly to the computer, or can have a communications link, either individually or shared, to an intermediate node in the network which electronically regulates and relays the transmissions over another channel to the still remote computer.

Installing a computer-based system in the library through networking has several advantages:

1. The library need not have a computer available locally in order to gain the benefits of a computer-based system; wherever a communications line can be installed in the library, a computer-based system shared with other libraries through a network can be used.
2. Usually, a shared system can be installed in the library within a few months or less.
3. As with a turnkey system, no time and money need be invested by the library in designing, programming, and testing the system.
4. The library need not have access to computer and systems specialists, because this expertise also is provided by the network organization or commercial firm.
5. If it is unhappy with the service or system provided by a network, the library can withdraw from participation with little loss of capital investment.
6. The network operations office usually assists in installing and maintaining essential hardware in the library and training the library staff to operate and manage the system.
7. While the library staff must learn to operate the in-house equipment and use the system, no special computer background is a prerequisite.

A potential disadvantage to sharing a computer-based system with other libraries through networking is that the individual library might feel as if it has little if anything to say about the services received; participating libraries usually must use the available services on a take-it-or-leave-it basis. Because many basic decisions are made by a network operations office or commercial firm, the individual library might feel a loss of control over important events that affect it.

Adapting Systems of Other Libraries. A library can duplicate and adapt another library's computer-based system for local installation and operation. The system can be installed to operate on an in-house computer or on one located outside the library but in its host institution or in a service bureau.

The primary advantage of this type of system is that the borrowing library can eliminate costly and time-consuming designing, programming, and testing because the originating library already will have performed these activities. However, there are some disadvantages:

1. The borrowed system will reflect all the policies and idiosyncracies of the original library, which may be different from those of the library wishing to use the system.

2. The borrowing library must have access to computer and systems specialists to adapt the application software to a local computer and install the system in the library.

3. More time and money could be spent in adapting another library's system than for another method of developing a system, with poorer results possible.

Developing Systems Locally from Scratch. The last method of developing a computer-based library system is to design, program, and test it locally from scratch. The application software is locally designed, programmed, tested, installed, operated, and maintained on an in-house computer or on one located outside the library but in its host institution or in a service bureau. The primary advantages to this method of developing a system include:

1. The system can be designed to meet the exact needs of the library.

2. Greater success probably will be achieved in integrating several systems together in the library.

3. The library can maintain control over all aspects of the system's development, installation, and operation.

However, this is the most difficult and time-consuming method of developing a system, with some additional disadvantages:

1. The library must have access to computer and systems specialists to design, program, test, and install the system.

2. Several years might pass before the library would have an operational system.

3. The library itself must acquire and maintain a computer system and other essential hardware or use equipment already available locally.

4. There is a general feeling that a library should not design again a system which many others already have developed and which could be obtained through other methods.

5. If all expenses are considered, the costs of developing, operating, and maintaining a system locally probably are as expensive as, if not more than, a turnkey or shared system, with poorer results possible.

ADVANTAGES AND DISADVANTAGES OF USING COMPUTER-BASED SYSTEMS

When properly designed, implemented, and managed, a computer-based system could offer many benefits or advantages to a library. However, such a system does have some limitations or disadvantages.

Advantages of Using Computer-Based Systems. Several general benefits can be realized by using a computer-based library system, including:

1. Reduced or at least stabilized operating costs of the system.
2. Capability to expand existing services and/or provide new services without additional staff and to improve performance times of operations—in other words, to perform more work with fewer people.
3. A shift of staff from performing undesirable tasks to performing more rewarding and stimulating duties.
4. Improved accountability for and control over informational materials, records, and services.

Specifically, a computer-based library system can:

1. Accept information in a digital form, accurately perform long sequences of repetitive, time-consuming operations on the input over a long period of time, and present the results of its processing to a user.
2. Store large amounts of information in mass storage devices and retrieve any or all of it on demand.
3. Operate at high speeds. Its speeds are measured in terms of milliseconds (one-thousandths of a second), microseconds (one-millionths of a second), nanoseconds (one-billionths of a second), and picoseconds (one-trillionths of a second).
4. Direct itself in a predetermined manner. The general-purpose digital computer has an internal storage unit or memory where information to be processed and interchangeable sets of processing instructions called *programs* are stored. Once it has been provided with information and instructions, there is no need for further human intervention and direction in the information processing cycle. The set of instructions can be removed or erased when others are required.
5. Choose among alternatives in processing information in a manner that is equivalent to making decisions. The computer makes comparisons of information, then follows paths dictated by the results.

6. Process one job at a time or several jobs almost simultaneously. By storing information and instructions for several jobs in different parts of its storage units and switching between them rapidly, the machine appears to be handling all jobs simultaneously.
7. Receive an input of information and instructions from users in remote locations via a data communications system, process the input, and transmit the results back to the user.

Disadvantages of Using Computer-Based Systems. There are limitations upon computer-based systems. In all cases the system is subject to human direction and control. For example, the computer can not:

1. Perform without programs. It must have a set of instructions for every application or job it is to perform, and every operation and decision to be made must be foreseen in advance and the alternatives specified in the programs. While it can perform at incredible speeds, the computer can do nothing that it is not programmed to do. It can perform no operation that can not be performed by humans.
2. Sense information unless it is in an acceptable form: that is, in a machine-readable form. This requires a conversion of symbolic information, which humans can readily understand, to machine language, which is the only language that a computer can understand. A computer can sense information only if it is in the form of electrical or electronic signals or pulses. Either a pulse is present or it is not; there is no in-between, and no other conditions are possible.
3. Operate on anything except information. It can accept information, process it, and communicate results, but the machine can not perform direct physical acts such as opening doors or turning pages of books. However, processed information can be used to control other machines or devices which can open doors or turn pages.
4. Correct inaccurate information fed into it. The results of computer processing are only as accurate as the input entered into the system.
5. Perform all necessary operations in most library systems. In all cases, humans must specify what information is to be collected and how it is to be organized, stored, retrieved, arranged and rearranged, and disseminated.

Chapter 2
Project Planning and Management

Some activities are necessary to plan and manage a project to develop a computer-based library system. Specifically, this chapter includes discussions of:

- The plan for project completion.
- The long-range plan for automation.
- The project manager.
- The project advisory committee.
- Project definition.
- Project approval.
- The project consultant.
- Other project resource people.

THE PLAN FOR PROJECT COMPLETION

A detailed plan for completing a project successfully must be prepared and approved. The plan usually consists of 3 parts or aspects: a project outline, a project schedule, and a method of reporting progress.

The Project Outline. A project is completed in stages called *phases*. Each phase contains a number of subdivisions called *activities,* and each activity comprises a number of *tasks* or *steps*. The exact number of events in a project depends upon the nature and complexity of the anticipated system to be developed and how it will be developed. A sample list of phases, activities, and steps for a project to develop a computer-based library system is shown in Appendix A.

An effective means of planning a project is to prepare an outline of the phases, activities, and steps which are expected to be accomplished in order to complete the endeavor successfully. The first level headings of the outline represent the phases of the project, the next level headings represent the activities of the project, and the third level headings represent steps of each activity, as shown in Appendix A.

The plan should be dynamic: that is, the outline can and must be altered as work on the project progresses and as new conditions and situations arise. For example, if, after the preliminary evaluation and comparison of systems have been completed, a commercially designed turnkey system is determined to be best for the library, then the outline must be revised to eliminate the now unnecessary design and programming activities of the project.

The Project Schedule. Either a simple Gantt chart or a network chart can be used as a means of scheduling and controlling the events in the project plan or outline.

The Gantt chart is one of the simplest and most effective scheduling tools (Figure 2-1). To prepare this chart, take the phases and/or activities to be completed from the project outline and list them along the left side of the chart. Time in days, weeks, or months is represented along the top. The expected or scheduled beginning and completion times of each event are indicated by Xs or a solid bar within the appropriate time frame. If desired, the actual beginning and completion times of each event can be shown beneath the expected times of each event. If this is done, those events which were started on time and are ahead or behind schedule can be quickly determined at a glance. A disadvantage to this type of chart is that it does not effectively indicate relationships among the different events of a project. Each time the project outline is changed, the chart also must be revised to reflect the changes.

A simple network chart graphically illustrates the interrelationships of events required to complete the work to be performed in a project. To prepare the chart, number the activities of a phase and draw a line between 2 circles to represent each activity. Place activities one after another from left to right. The sequence of the activities shown on the chart represents the sequence in which they should or must be completed; in most cases, an activity can not be started until a previous one has been completed. If 2 or more activities can be completed simultaneously, separate lines emanating from the same circle are drawn. A series of network charts for the activities shown in Appendix A are shown in Appendix B.

The network chart can also be used as a scheduling tool if beginning and completion times are estimated and added to the activities. Program evaluation and review technique (PERT) and critical path method (CPM) are other similar networking tools useful in planning, scheduling, and controlling a project. While these are not described here, references to other literature can be found in the bibliography to this book.

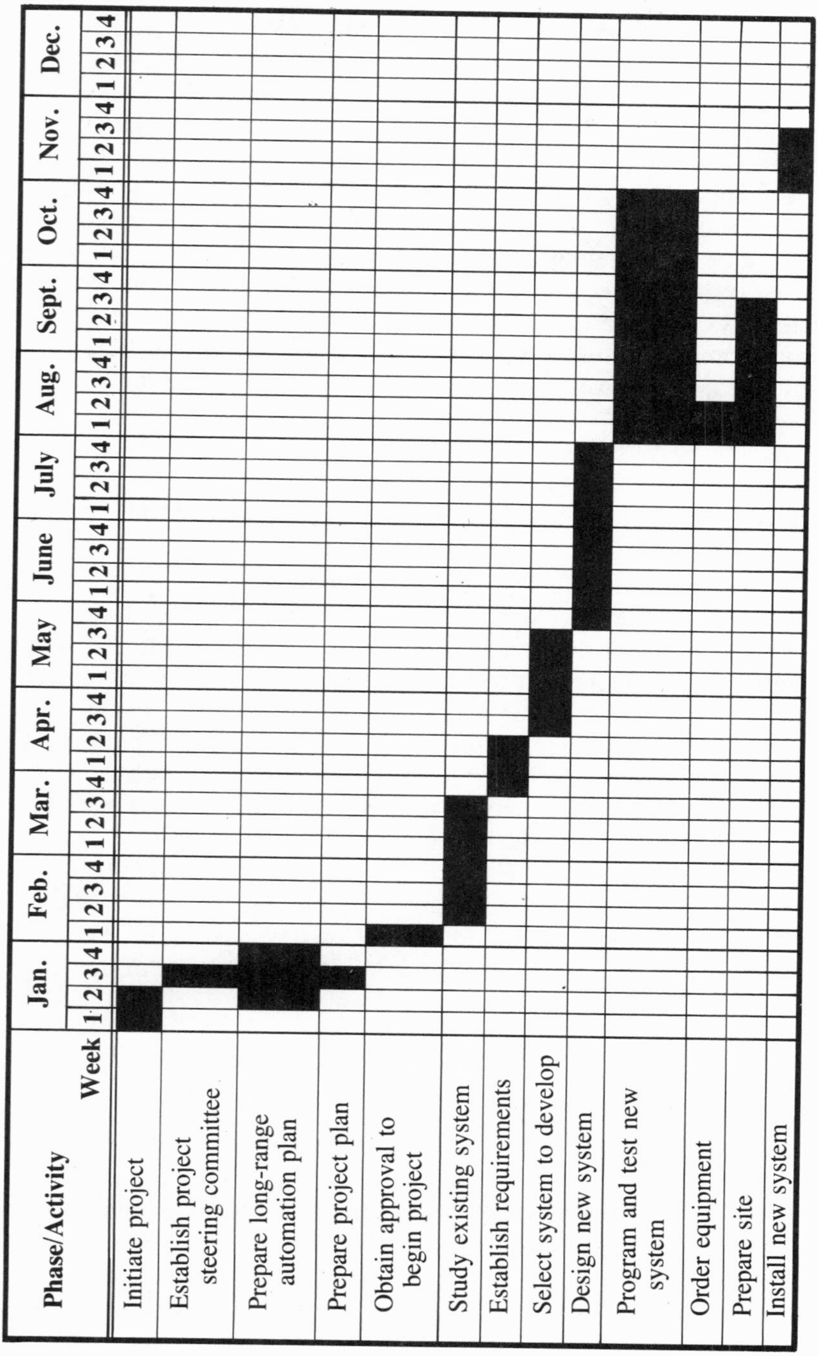

Figure 2-1. A Gantt chart used as a project schedule.

<u>Progress Reports</u>. A means should be established to report regularly the progress being made towards completion of the project to the library director, the project advisory committee, and others. Wide distribution of the project plan or outline and the current project schedule provides an excellent method of informing others about the endeavor. In addition, every opportunity should be taken to discuss the project informally with others and present verbal reports at meetings with the library director, governing and funding authorities, and others. Written progress reports based on the project outline and schedule also can be issued at regular intervals. The reports should include, as a minimum, short descriptions of work completed to-date compared with estimated completion times and any unexpected problems encountered since the last report.

THE LONG-RANGE PLAN FOR AUTOMATION

It behooves the library not to allow computer-based systems within its organization to be developed in isolation from each other. If a long-range or master plan for automating the library does not exist, one should be prepared before a project to develop the first computer-based system is begun. Such a plan becomes a blueprint for future planning of library services using computer and related technology. As many people as possible from all areas of the library should be involved in developing the plan. The development of as many systems as possible should be planned at the same time, although implementation of individual systems can proceed one at a time as time and funds permit. Each new system to be developed should be required to be compatible with all other systems in the library, and adequate documentation for all that are developed should be provided so that a written record of past work will be available in the future. A long-range plan should include as a minimum:

1. A mission statement for the library as an organization.
2. A goals or purpose statement for automation.
3. A list of any requirements or constraints to be placed on automation projects.
4. An anticipated schedule and priority list for developing individual computer-based systems in the library.

A sample long-range plan for a library's automation program is shown in Appendix C.

THE PROJECT MANAGER

Responsibility for the successful completion of a project to develop a computer-based system must be delegated to one person referred to as the *project coordinator, director,* or *manager.* Whether the project manager is selected and appointed before or after a project has been defined depends upon circumstances and personal preference. Even if a consultant is to be hired to develop a new system, someone on the library staff should be appointed to serve as a project manager to work with and serve as a liaison to the consultant.

If several projects requiring many years to complete are anticipated, a department or office responsible solely for systems planning, improvement, and development might be established within the library organization. The responsibilities of such a permanent unit might include the management of specific projects to improve present systems and the development of new ones. An advantage to this arrangement is that this staff can devote the time necessary to a project, because developing new systems will be one reason that the department exists. A disadvantage is that one or more staff positions must be created, funded, filled, and housed.

In most small libraries, responsibility for development of computer-based library systems must be given to someone who will be temporarily relieved of other duties until the completion of the project. Responsibility for a project can be assigned to an associate or assistant director or to a staff member in technical or public services, depending upon the type of system to be developed. In some cases, management of the project must be added to other duties of a staff member. The advantage to this approach is that a new staff position need not be created, funded, filled, and housed. The obvious disadvantage is that the person will be taken from other duties which might suffer.

The person chosen as project manager should have a broad knowledge of the library organization and its operations and staff, in addition to other specific abilities. A project manager should be able to:

1. Think creatively and logically and with an open mind to new and fresh ideas.

2. Grasp the fundamentals and perplexing terminology of systems, computer hardware and software, and data communications.

3. Communicate and work effectively with library staff, vendors, programmers, and others who would be assisting in development of a system.

4. Understand and cope with the complexity of small details neces-sary to complete a project.
5. Sell a new system to governing and funding authorities and to a possibly apprehensive staff who might fear change and loss of prestige or their jobs.
6. Maintain schedules and meet deadlines.

The specific duties or responsibilities of the project manager will depend upon her or his background and capabilities and the nature of the undertaking. The project manager could have to:

1. Analyze an assignment and determine what must be accom-plished to complete a project successfully.
2. Organize, coordinate, and direct the day-to-day work required to complete a project within an established time schedule and budget.
3. Establish and maintain communication and negotiate with, and serve as a liaison and resource person to, hardware and software vendors, programmers, and others not on the library staff but who will be contributing to the successful development of a system.
4. Analyze and study existing operations in order to determine needs for a new system.
5. Identify, compare, and evaluate alternative systems and recom-mend for development the best system to meet the library's needs.
6. If necessary, design a system to best meet identified needs of the library.
7. Develop hardware and software specifications for a new system.
8. Produce documentation for a new system.
9. Recommend and provide training for staff who will operate and manage a new system.
10. Coordinate new system installation and solve problems which are encountered in that activity.
11. Serve as a resource person in general to the library staff for information about computer hardware, software, and systems.
12. Keep the library director and other staff informed about a proj-ect's progress and problems.

The manager should report directly to the library director in regard to a project, thus emphasizing the importance of the work, enabling the library director to maintain control over this important work, and enabling all departments of the library to be served equally, impartially, and free from control of any one unit.

THE PROJECT ADVISORY COMMITTEE

The formation of an advisory committee can provide an excellent means of involving staff and insuring the development of a better computer-based system. However, it should be emphasized that the project manager remains ultimately responsible for the successful completion of a project, and thus must assume responsibility for the final decisions.

The specific duties or responsibilities of the advisory committee depend upon the nature of the project to be undertaken. Typical duties of this group might include:

1. Assisting in the establishment of objectives, requirements, and specifications for a new system to be developed.
2. Assisting in the selection of the best system to be developed.
3. Assisting in the selection of a project consultant, if one is needed.
4. Providing the project manager with general advice and guidance during the new system development process.
5. Providing general support for the project and for a new system to be developed.

Once the duties of the committee are established, its members can be selected and appointed. The committee can consist of key staff of a present system and those who will manage and operate the new system once it has been developed. The size of the committee probably should not be fewer than 3 nor more than 5 or 6 members; a smaller number would negate the committee concept and a larger number would be too unwieldy. While the project manager can suggest names of prospective committee members, the library director should make the appointments of those who will serve, to stress the importance attached to the committee. The project manager might be an ex officio member of the committee, but probably should not serve as its chairman.

PROJECT DEFINITION

A project to develop a computer-based library system should be clearly defined before its initiation is formally requested. Project definition usually consists of at least 3 parts: problem definition, project objectives, and project constraints.

Problem Definition. A problem or problems facing the library usually underlie the need for developing a new or improved library system. These problems can be identified through personal observations and knowledge of situations, reports from other staff, results of studies of the library, or suggestions and complaints from users. For example, some problems which might cause a library to seek a better system are that:

1. Work in an existing system is increasing so rapidly that the increased volume can not be handled effectively.
2. Costs in an existing system are increasing rapidly.
3. Pressures from funding officials, taxpayers, and others are mounting for the library to perform more work with fewer staff members and to provide better accountability for materials and services in the future.
4. An existing system is not flexible enough to accommodate new functions, ideas, or services that must be incorporated into the library.
5. An existing system needs improvement in general. The system might be operating satisfactorily but is limited in what it can do and unable to provide, for example, adequate administrative reports and statistics.

Symptoms of problems may be more readily apparent at first than the problems themselves. For example, some symptoms of problems might be:

1. Increased times required to process materials.
2. Long queues at service desks.
3. An increasing number of errors in a system or service.
4. A decline in the quality of a service.
5. A high number of complaints from users.
6. An awareness that users are turning more frequently to other organizations for information services.
7. A continual need for more funds.
8. A necessary curtailment of services due to lack of staff, time, or funds.

Once symptoms are identified, their causes can be explored to determine the problems. The facts that a computer is available, that free computer time is offered to the library, that the project initiator thinks using a computer will make the library appear progressive, or that other libraries use computers are not sound, legitimate reasons for the development of a new system; each of these is the equivalent of saying, "Here's a solution—now let's find a problem that fits it."

Problems which are identified should be translated into clear, unambiguous, specific statements. A problem statement should include:

1. A brief description of the problem.
2. What has happened as a result of the problem.
3. Supporting costs, work measures and other quantitative facts and statistics.

For example, a problem might be stated in this manner:

Because of increased use of the library and the resulting increased number of loans to borrowers without a corresponding increase in personnel, the circulation staff must spend almost its entire time charging and discharging materials.

The results of the example problem could be:

As a result of the problem, long service queues form at the charge station; long delays in discharging materials occur; all except first overdue notices have had to be eliminated; large backlogs of records awaiting merging into the circulation file are frequent; and low morale of the staff resulting from complaints from borrowers about slow service has developed.

And the supporting data could be as follows:

	Persons Using Library	Number of Loans	Staff
1975	40,000	110,980	4.0
1976	65,500	156,777	4.0
1977	91,900	209,080	4.5
1978	111,500	224,523	4.5
1979	124,800	260,129	4.5

As another example, a problem might be stated in this manner:

Because of the increased number of materials purchased and a mandated reduction of staff, the catalog department staff can process only 60 percent of the library's new acquisitions each year.

The results of the example problem could be:

As a result of this problem, the backlog of materials awaiting processing is increasing rapidly; users are unable to have speedy access to new materials; the number of processing errors has increased due to the pressures to handle more materials; and low morale of the staff resulting from complaints from users about the slow processing times has developed.

And the supporting data:

	Titles Added	Staff	Titles in Backlog	Average Processing Time in Days
1975	31,580	8.0	2,000	42.0
1976	38,890	7.5	4,500	55.7
1977	42,300	7.0	6,900	61.8
1978	45,672	6.5	8,500	68.0
1979	49,858	6.5	9,000	72.3

As a last example, a problem might be stated as:

The acquisitions department must begin reporting to the library commit-tee each month the number and cost of titles acquired by requesting agency or department. Also, a new accounting system to meet new fiscal requirements mandated by the city (or county or state) must be installed.

The results of the example problem could be:

The present system cannot report the new statistics without additional staff or an elimination of other services, due to the time-consuming nature of gathering, compiling, and reporting the desired information. Also, integrating the new accounting system into the existing system will necessitate a complete overhaul of all procedures from submission of requests for purchase through receipt and payment of invoices.

In this example, no specific supporting data were available. Statistical and accounting reports and other budgetary information can be studied and analyzed to obtain the supporting data. Including quantitative facts and statistics provides a means by which a reader can quickly assess the need for a solution to a problem. Including cost or other supporting data for several years is preferable to stating only that, for example, the average cost of circulating an item is now $3.78 per transac-tion, because a reader would have nothing to which this limited informa-tion can be related; and is better than stating vaguely that the cost of providing a service is increasing too fast, because the reader would have no way of judging what "too fast" means.

Another approach to documenting the need for a project is simply to identify and list the problems underlying the situation. For example, some problems documenting the need for a new circulation system might in-clude, among others:

1. The staff required to perform the circulation activities is increasing and user waiting periods for service are increasing.

2. The present system does not enable staff to determine what mate-rials are charged to which borrowers.

3. Overdue notices cannot be sent regularly on schedule.

4. The circulation statistics are often inaccurate and untimely and insufficient for managerial purposes.

5. Recalls and holds cannot be placed.

6. Fine collection transactions cannot be reconciled with cash drawer receipts.

Project Objectives. Once one or more problems have been identified, defined, and documented, the problem statements can be used to formulate objectives for the project.

While the purpose or purposes of a project might appear obvious, a written statement can assist in eliminating any ambiguity or uncertainty and provide a reference and focal point for the work to be undertaken. Like the problem statement, the statement of objectives should be clear, unambiguous, and specific. It outlines the end results towards which achievements should be directed or specifies what is expected to be accomplished or achieved in an endeavor to develop a new system. Quantification of the statement can be helpful in guiding development of a new system and evaluating it later to determine if the objective was met. For example, some objectives for a project might be to:

1. Upgrade and improve the effectiveness and efficiency of the present circulation system.
2. Obtain a new or improved bibliographic control system which will enable the staff to process 100 percent of the library's new acquisitions each year.
3. Upgrade the effectiveness of the present acquisitions system, with specific purposes to:
   a. Reduce the time and difficulty of acquiring new materials.
   b. Improve and simplify procedures.
   c. Provide complete accountability for materials from selection through receipt and processing.
   d. Reduce the per unit cost of acquiring materials by 10 percent over the present system.
   e. Eliminate all manual files.
   f. Provide better control over materials being acquired.
   g. Reduce the per unit operating costs of acquiring materials.
   h. Reduce the staff required to acquire materials by 50 percent.
   i. Provide accurate statistics of materials being acquired and accurate accounting of materials funds.

Project Constraints. Project constraints are limits or conditions which are placed on a project. For example, a project might be required to be completed by a certain date and within a set budget; to use particular techniques or staff during a project; to receive approval of the library director before each new phase of the project is begun; and to concentrate on developing an online system only. Constraints can be identified through personal knowledge of situations, discussions with library staff and others, and examinations of library policies and other legal documents.

PROJECT APPROVAL

The library director should have either formally or informally authorized the initiation of the project and completion of the project plan. Higher governing or funding authorities may or may not have been involved up to this point. Before further work is performed, formal approval to initiate the project should be sought and granted.

A report document can be prepared for submission to the library director and others for formal approval to initiate the project. The document should be brief yet complete and clear enough for easy assessment of the merits of approving the undertaking to continue. The information in this document should include as a minimum:

1. A statement of the purposes and/or objectives of the project.
2. The problem statement which underlies the need for a project and, therefore, a new system.
3. A statement of any constraints placed on the project.
4. Identification of the project manager and a list of the members of the project advisory committee, if one is to be used, and, if desired, their duties or responsibilities.
5. A summary outline of the plan for completing the project successfully.

Other pertinent background or explanatory information which the project manager feels necessary to improve the report can be added. A sample document prepared to seek approval to initiate a project is shown in Appendix D.

A draft of the report can be circulated widely before it is submitted for approval, in order to inform the library staff of the impending request for approval, solicit their suggestions for improving the document, and gain their vital support for the endeavor and any new or improved system which might result. Formal or informal meetings and discussions can be held to gain input from as many of the staff as possible. Their suggestions and comments should be evaluated carefully and, if possible, incorporated into the document before it is submitted for approval.

After it has been approved by the library director, the report must be presented to the city manager, mayor, president, board, council, or other group advising or governing the library for their authorization or approval to proceed with the project. Even if persons or groups have advisory powers only, their approval should be sought and obtained before work on a project continues. These people will be instrumental later in obtaining needed funds for a new or improved system.

If the project is small, authorization for its completion may be granted outright; but, usually, instructions are given to conduct a preliminary or feasibility study before a decision is made whether or not to continue the project. It should be emphasized to those authorizing the project that its initiation does not necessarily commit the library to developing a computer-based system or mean that one should be developed. The result of the feasibility study could be that development of a computer-based system is not feasible, cannot be justified economically, and should not be pursued. In this case, the project can be terminated and the existing system retained in perhaps a streamlined and simplified form. On the other hand, the preliminary study might indicate that a computer-based system is feasible, can be justified economically, and should be developed. It must be emphasized again that whether or not a computer-based system can be economically justified cannot be determined until a preliminary or feasibility study is conducted.

THE PROJECT CONSULTANT

A consultant or consulting firm can be hired to conduct a feasibility or preliminary study, prepare design specifications for a new system, or manage a project from beginning to end. A consultant might be needed if no one on the library staff has the specialized background and skills essential to perform all activities of a project, no one on the staff can be spared to perform all the necessary activities, or it is thought that an outside person would be more objective in performing some activities of a project. A project manager still is necessary to coordinate the work in general, be responsible for the successful completion of the project, and serve as a liaison between the consultant and the library staff and others.

A request for information (RFI), request for quotation (RFQ), or request for proposal (RFP), hereafter referred to generally as a request for proposal or RFP, should be prepared to secure a project consultant. Usually, the project manager and the project advisory committee jointly prepare this document, which serves as a means of advertising that the library is seeking a consultant, provides prospective consultants with necessary information about the work to be performed, and solicits information from those who submit proposals to perform the work.

An RFP should be brief but clear and concise, with the following as the minimum information to be included:

1. A general narrative description of the library and its environment.
2. A summary description of the project being undertaken.

3. A detailed statement of the work the consultant is to perform. The anticipated results also can be specified.
4. A description of written and verbal reports expected from the consultant.
5. An outline of information required in proposals from prospective consultants in response to the RFP. The library should request from each consultant submitting a proposal:
   a. A proposed methodology and the amount of time anticipated to complete the work specified in the RFP.
   b. The total cost bid for performing the work, including costs for all staff time, supplies, travel, per diem, and other miscellaneous costs.
   c. The names and qualifications or brief resumes of all persons who will assist in performing the contracted work for the library.
   d. The names and addresses of libraries that have used the consultant's services in the past.
6. The methodology the library will use to select the consultant to be hired.
7. The anticipated calendar for the project, including deadlines for submitting proposals to the library and the date the library expects to select the successful bidder.
8. The name, address, and telephone number of the project manager or other person who can be contacted for additional information about the project or RFP.

A sample request for proposal for securing a project consultant can be found in Appendix E.

Once an RFP has been prepared and approved by the project advisory committee and others, copies must be distributed to solicit proposals from prospective consultants. There are several methods of identifying consultants to whom the RFP can be sent, including:

1. Asking the American Library Association, other professional organizations, or the state library to provide a list of possible consultants.
2. Asking colleagues and friends if they can recommend one or more consultants.
3. Advertising by word of mouth or by placing notices on bulletin boards at local, state, regional, or national professional meetings.
4. Reading the professional literature to identify consultants or writers on automation in the area of the library's project who potentially might serve as a consultant.

A combination of approaches might be necessary to compile a mailing list for soliciting bids. A brief letter explaining why the RFP is being sent to a prospective consultant can be included.

Once proposals have been received, the best consultant for the project should be chosen on the basis of a combination of factors, including:

1. The best proposed methodology for completing the project.
2. The best time schedule for completing the project.
3. Satisfactory results achieved for other libraries in consulting assignments.
4. Whether or not the staff feels it can work easily with the consultant.
5. The costs bid to complete the work successfully.

The project manager and advisory committee should examine, compare, and evaluate the proposals received from prospective consultants. Additional or clarifying information can be requested from a bidder if necessary, and telephone or in-person interviews may be held with several of the best candidates before a final decision is made. Inquiries should be made to several or all the libraries that have used a prospective consultant's services in the past, and on-site visits can be made to the libraries if they are nearby. Reports and other documentation produced for these libraries should be examined if possible.

After the best proposal has been selected and the successful bidder has been notified, the project manager should have a simple contract drawn up and signed by the consultant and a legal representative of the library. As a courtesy, the unsuccessful bidders should be notified of the bid award and thanked for submitting proposals.

OTHER PROJECT RESOURCE PEOPLE

The talents of many people other than the project manager, project advisory committee, and project consultant are required in the development of a computer-based library system. Many will not be on the library staff. Some people who may play important roles in a project include:

1. The library director.
2. Staff of an existing system.
3. Staff of a computer center.
4. Hardware and software vendors.
5. Staff in other automated libraries.
6. Representatives of library networks.
7. Miscellaneous personnel.

Library Director. The role of the library director in a project to develop a computer-based library system should be that of an overseer, a critic, an advisor, and an encourager and enthusiast. The director should provide continuing support for the project and its manager; give approval when necessary to decisions made by the project manager and advisory committee; keep governing and funding authorities apprised of progress being made in developing the new system; and secure approval and funding for the new system from governing and funding authorities. The director might initiate the project and appoint its manager and advisory committee, but she or he will not normally be directly involved in the day-to-day activities of the endeavor; that is the function of the project manager.

Staff of an Existing System. While the project advisory committee provides most of the guidance for development of a new system, other staff of the existing system can be solicited when necessary for information about operations as they currently are being performed and suggestions for their improvement. These people can provide valuable information about the present system and needs and demands for a new one. Since the ultimate success of a new system depends to a great extent upon the support and interest given it by those who will operate and manage it, these people will be more prone to accept a new system if they feel personally involved in its development and if they can see tangible benefits to them and to the library. Their continuing involvement in the project can facilitate their support and approval of any new or improved system which will be implemented. A new system suddenly imposed upon the rank and file staff without their prior knowledge or involvement may not be easily and readily accepted.

Staff of a Computer Center. Most libraries now have access to a central data processing or computer center serving their host institution or organization. The center might consist of one or several computer systems, communications equipment for distributing computing power to remote locations, data conversion equipment such as keypunches or CRT terminals, and other peripheral hardware essential to maintain and operate the installation.

The specialized staff who operate and manage this center can be very helpful in providing and interpreting information about computers and assisting the library in planning, designing, implementing, and operating a computer-based system. Even if it does not plan to use the center's computer systems, the library can benefit from the knowledge, advice, and political weight of its staff.

The director or manager of the computer center, who usually reports directly to the president of an academic institution or corporation or to the city manager in a city government, can provide the library staff with general information about computer hardware, software, and systems and with specific information about the center's equipment and services.

The systems analysts on the computer center staff can assist the library in analyzing existing systems, planning and designing new systems, and adapting systems borrowed from other libraries. If the library plans to develop a computer-based system locally from scratch or adapt a system borrowed from another library, the center's programmers can provide assistance in designing, coding, debugging, testing, and installing the necessary system software.

Hardware and Software Vendors. Representatives of hardware and software vendors can provide valuable assistance by supplying information about products which the library is considering for acquisition and later by supplying the actual products. The librarian must remember, however, that these representatives are trying to sell products and their views will be biased in favor of the equipment or techniques their firms are manufacturing and/or marketing.

Vendor representatives usually are pleased to provide descriptive brochures and other information about their products, and, if requested, most will visit the library at no obligation in order to provide additional verbal and visual information and perhaps demonstrate their products. Also, most vendors attempting to reach the library market exhibit their systems at national, regional, and state library conventions. On such occasions the librarian can see the equipment, have the systems demonstrated, talk with vendor representatives, obtain informational brochures, and possibly talk with other librarians who use these products.

Staff in Other Automated Libraries. The staff of other libraries with computer-based systems can be helpful by demonstrating their systems and sharing experiences encountered during their projects. Advice about systems development and problems which will be encountered or to be avoided can be helpful to the library which does not yet have experience with computer-based systems. Often, encouragement from the staff in another automated library benefits the library just beginning to develop its first computer-based system.

Representatives of Library Networks. If a computer-based system is to be shared with others through a national, interstate, or intrastate network, representatives of the network's organization can supply promotional literature, technical information, and demonstrations to assist in the decision whether the system should be developed in the library. Once the decision has been made to develop a computer-based system through networking, the network representatives can assist in integrating the system into existing operations in the library and can provide some or all of the staff training essential to use the new system.

Miscellaneous Personnel. Perhaps hundreds of other people will be involved in development of a computer-based library system, including purchasing agents; legal advisors; communications experts; carpenters; electronics engineers; electrical engineers and technicians; air conditioning and heating experts; painters; hardware and software installers and maintenance staff; typists and clerical staff to prepare requests for proposals or quotations; data entry staff for file conversion projects; training staff for teaching the staff to operate and manage the new system; and many others. Each will play a vital role in the process of planning, designing, and implementing a computer-based system in the library.

Chapter 3
New System Requirements

A critical part of a project is the establishment of requirements for the new system to be developed for the library. A system requirement specifies what a system must do or how it must be designed in order to satisfy the needs of the library. It also may limit or restrict the system's design, operation, or performance in some manner.

The purpose of establishing system requirements is to obtain a clear picture of the system wanted before the available alternatives are examined and one is selected for development. Without this effort, the project manager can only guess as to the needs and desires of the library management and staff for a new system. An analogy might be a contractor who is told to begin building a new house without a set of blueprints and that specifications will be provided as construction progresses. A poorer house—or system—will result unless the expected end product is envisioned and planned before construction begins.

Once established, a set of requirements are used:

1. To identify systems which possibly might meet the needs of the library.

2. To compare and evaluate the alternatives which are identified.

3. To communicate in later phases of the project with library management and staff, governing authorities, vendors, programmers, and others as to the exact needs and desires for a new system.

4. To guide the later preparation of more detailed specifications for the new system.

5. To evaluate the new system, once it has been developed and installed, to determine if it is operating as anticipated and meeting the needs established at the beginning of the project.

Specifically, this chapter includes discussions of:

- An analysis of an existing system.
- Goals of the new system.
- Development of the set of requirements.
- General requirements.
- Functional requirements.
- Work and performance requirements.

ANALYSIS OF THE EXISTING SYSTEM

Because of the tendency to transfer old methods to the new, thereby stifling a fresh approach to the development process, the staff perhaps will more creatively establish new system requirements if they know little about the old system to be replaced. However, an analysis of specific aspects of an existing system can enable the staff to identify problems with the current situation and understand the existing system well enough to form the foundation for a better one; therefore, it is a helpful starting point in establishing requirements for the new system to be developed.

The analysis—some prefer to call it a description—consists of collecting, organizing, and analyzing facts about the existing system's goals, input and output, processing operations, resources, and environment. A wide range of analytical tools is available. Both detailed descriptions of the tools and instructions for their use occur in the literature of systems analysis. (See the bibliography to this book for selected references.)

The following elements of systems analysis are described briefly:

- The system's goals or purposes.
- Subsystems of the system.
- The system's documents and files.
- The system's work flow.
- The amount of work performed in the system.
- The resources required by the system.
- The system's physical space.
- Costs of operating the system.
- Organization of the results for later use.

The System's Goals or Purposes. The goals or purposes of the existing system should be identified and documented. Sometimes, these goals are well thought out and in writing; more often, the goals of a system being analyzed are implied, unstated, and rarely, if ever, referred to. The implied but unstated goals of the system should be verbalized and documented through interviews with the system's managers and staff.

Subsystems of the System. A list or diagram of the functional areas or subsystems of the system being studied provides an overview of the system and serves as a beginning and focal point for further analysis and for organizing new system requirements. The block diagram (see Figure 5-1) provides one of the best methods of graphically depicting the functional areas or subsystems of a system and enables the analyst to separate or divide a large complex system into smaller, more manageable parts which can be more readily studied. The goals or purposes of each subsystem also can be identified and documented. These goals must support rather than conflict with the overall goals of the system as a whole in order to avoid wasting resources.

The System's Documents and Files. An inventory and analysis of all forms, records, and reports used for the collection, input, processing, storage, and output of information and of all files maintained and used in each subsystem can be helpful in the analysis. An information usage chart (see Figure 5-4) can be prepared to summarize the individual forms, records, and reports and the pieces of information contained in each. This chart provides an overview of the information required by the system being analyzed and shows the overlap or duplication of information among the forms, records, and reports used. The chart also can provide a means of identifying the files and describing each in detail and will be invaluable later in preparing requirements and specifications for the files needed in the new system to be developed.

The System's Work Flow. The flow of work through the subsystems of the system being studied can be mapped and charted. The decision flowchart (Appendix H) provides one of the best methods of graphically depicting work flow. These flowcharts can provide graphic or pictorial representations of the input, processes performed on input, the sequences of processing steps, and output of the subsystems. Preparation of the charts forces a thorough understanding of the area under study and quickly reveals gaps in knowledge about it. They also enable unnecessary or duplicative processes, bottlenecks, and breaks in continuity of work flow to be spotted. Since the charts are widely used and understood, they can be a medium of communication between the analyst and others who wish to understand the system. Additional descriptions of flowcharts can be found in chapter 5.

The Amount of Work Performed in the System. The amount of work performed in each subsystem should be determined and documented. The work performed in a circulation system, for example, might include the number of charges, discharges, renewals, and holds or recalls completed during a year. Past statistical reports generated by the system can be examined and analyzed to obtain the type and volume of work performed.

If no statistics have been retained for work performed, a sampling can be taken. Work sampling involves observing work being performed at random times. From these random observations, the volume of work can be extrapolated or predicted. Estimates of the amount of work performed also can be made, but this method is less precise than the actual report analysis or sampling.

The Resources Required by the System. An inventory of personnel, equipment, and supplies necessary to operate and maintain the system can be prepared. No special forms are necessary to list these resources.

The System's Physical Space. A layout chart for the system being studied can be prepared to graphically or pictorially represent the physical space in which the system is operated, with work areas and their related furniture and equipment shown. This chart is very similar to that in Figure 3-5 except that the flow lines are omitted. The diagram can aid the analyst in visualizing the location and relationship of work areas of the system and locating traffic patterns and congestion. Later, the chart can be used in planning the space to house the new system.

Costs of Operating the System. Cost figures for operating and maintaining the system should be gathered and documented. The results of this study are used to compare the existing system with alternatives which might replace it. Additional information on costs can be found in chapter 4.

Organization of Results for Later Use. Once a study of an existing system has been completed, the results should be organized so that the information can be located easily and used in later activities of the project. The information gathered about the system can be placed into folders or a binder under the following topics:

1. System goals or purposes.
2. System subsystems and their goals or purposes.
3. Files, forms, records, and reports.
4. Work flow.
5. Work measurement.
6. System resources.
7. Physical space.
8. Costs.
9. Miscellaneous, such as general descriptive and background information, copies of organizational charts, policy and procedure manuals or memoranda, statistical reports, monthly and annual reports, and reports of any previous analyses or studies.

GOALS OF THE NEW SYSTEM

The statement of goals should include the purpose of the new system or achievements toward which efforts in developing, maintaining, and operating it will be directed. The goals statement can be based on that of an existing system or can be completely new. For example, the goals of a new acquisitions system might be:

1. To acquire books, periodicals, documents, audiovisual, and other materials effectively and efficiently for the library's collections through purchases, gifts, and exchanges.
2. To provide a reliable means of controlling and reporting the expenditure of acquisitions funds.

The project manager can draft the new set of goals for staff consideration and approval. Once accepted, the statement will provide a focus for the project advisory committee and others in their development of the new system requirements. The statement can be refined and changed as specifications for the new system are proposed.

DEVELOPMENT OF THE SET OF REQUIREMENTS

Members of the project advisory committee and other interested persons can be asked to compile lists of their specific needs, desires, and demands to be placed on the new system to be developed. The lists should be as detailed as possible, in order to provide as complete a picture of the system wanted as possible. Each requirement should be clear and unambiguous and labeled as being either *mandatory* or *desirable*. A mandatory requirement is one which absolutely must be met by the design of the new system, while a desirable requirement may enhance the system but need not necessarily be met for a system to be acceptable.

The lists of requirements submitted by the staff can be consolidated into a master list and edited into a draft set of requirements for the new system, then circulated for additional comments and suggestions. The project advisory committee should discuss, refine, and change the requirements until a realistic, clear definition of the system wanted for the library emerges. It might be necessary to draft, edit, and circulate several lists before the project manager and advisory committee accept and approve a working set of requirements. The final set should have consensus approval and acceptance of the project manager, the advisory committee, the library director, and other concerned persons. Further refinements and changes can be made to the list as work on the project progresses.

A single list of requirements can be prepared or the list can be divided into categories such as those below. Other categories can be developed if necessary or desired. A sample set of requirements for a new computer-based circulation system is shown in Appendix F.

GENERAL REQUIREMENTS

General requirements define and establish broad guidelines for the new computer-based system. Requirements of this type usually pertain to system flexibility, compatibility, control, and cost.

Flexibility Requirements. Flexibility requirements describe the extent to which the new system must be adaptable to meet future conditions without complete redesign or noticeable disruption of its operations. For example:

1. The new system must be designed so that, after it is installed and operational, it can be modified without complete redesign or noticeable disruption of service when library policies must be changed, new hardware and techniques must be adopted, or unforeseen problems in system operation suddenly occur.

2. The new system must be designed to handle eventually up to 25 branches or collection locations, 25,000 borrowers, 500,000 unique titles, and 1,000,000 individual copies without new hardware and software.

Compatibility Requirements. Compatibility requirements define how the new system is to interface with other systems. Systems are compatible if the output of one can be accepted as input by another and processed successfully to achieve a desired result. Also, the systems with which the new system must be compatible should be identified. For example:

1. The new system must be compatible with the city's automated accounting system.

2. The new system must be compatible with all other automated systems in the library.

3. The new system must be compatible with the circulation systems in neighboring libraries in the city, county, or region.

4. The new system must be compatible with the policies and procedures of a national organization such as OCLC, etc.

Control Requirements. Control requirements specify and define any regulations and constraints placed on the new system due to laws, regulations, recommendations, or policies of library management, governing authorities, or others. For example:

1. The new system must provide an auditable hardcopy of all fines collected.
2. The new system must protect the privacy of all individuals.
3. The new system must provide for the date-dues provided for in the library's circulation policies.

Cost Requirements. Cost requirements specify any cost constraints on the new system. For example:

1. The costs of operating the new system must not be more than the manual system it replaces.
2. The new system must reduce operating costs after a specified length of time.
3. Developmental costs must not exceed a specified amount.

The availability of funds obviously can dictate the type of system which can be developed and therefore can limit the quantity and quality of its output. Few, if any, libraries are given carte blanche to develop a new computer-based system without some cost constraints stipulated.

FUNCTIONAL REQUIREMENTS

The bulk of the list of requirements for the new system will be of a functional nature, defining specifically what the new system must be able to do. To facilitate conceptualization of these requirements, the new system can be separated into subsystems, if desired, and separate lists of functional requirements can be established for each area. For example, a system or subsystem can be required to be able to:

1. Create records for up to 15 types of borrowers.
2. Update information about old borrowers.
3. Maintain borrower records in a database.
4. Identify borrowers with expired registration dates.
5. Format and print registration notices to borrowers.
6. Process errors in data entry.
7. Format and print lists of borrowers by their type.

The list should be as detailed as possible for each subsystem, in order to provide a complete picture of the new system wanted.

WORK AND PERFORMANCE REQUIREMENTS

Work and performance requirements specify the expected amount of work to be accomplished by the new system during a period of time such as a day, week, month, or year and the speed with which transactions or operations must be completed by the new system. Past statistical records generated by the existing system can be examined and analyzed to obtain the type and volume of work to be performed. The time duration of each type of work should be stated; all should be stated in the same amount of time if possible. For example, requirements for a new circulation system can be established that the new system must be able to handle:

- 10,000 new borrower registrations per year.
- 22,000 registration notices per year.
- 100,000 charge transactions made per year.
- 52,000 renewals made per year.
- 9,800 holds placed each year.
- 2,500 recalls made per year.
- $52,182 fines collected each year from 14,050 borrowers.
- 98,250 overdue notices sent each year.

Examples of timing requirements could be that:

1. The new system must have an average response time of 5 seconds or less for inquiries.
2. The new system must have an average response time of 3 seconds or less for charges, discharges, and renewals.

Chapter 4
System Evaluation and Comparison

It is likely that several, if not many, systems could be developed for a particular library. A study often is necessary to evaluate and compare the alternatives available and select the best system for development. Most libraries would not be allowed to continue with a project until such a study has been conducted and a summary report written and accepted by the library's management and governing and funding authorities. A consultant can be retained to evaluate and compare the available alternatives, but the project manager can perform the work with similar results.

Specifically, this chapter includes discussions of:

- Decision rules for selecting the best system.
- The list of alternative systems to be considered.
- Comparison of alternatives to requirements.
- Comparison of developmental costs.
- Comparison of operating costs.
- Selection of the best system.
- Documentation of the results.

DECISION RULES FOR SELECTING THE BEST SYSTEM

The computer-based system to be developed by the library should be the one which most closely matches a set of criteria or decision rules established before a comparison of the alternatives is begun. A decision rule is a policy by which to judge the best alternative system being considered, or a standard against which each system is evaluated; thus, it provides an intelligent basis upon which to select one system over another.

The rules must be based on accurate knowledge of the internal and external constraints upon the library, which usually include pressures or policies from library management, a governing body, staff, or users to perform the most work in the shortest possible time at the least cost while maintaining quality standards. The following are examples of common decision rules for selecting the best system during an evaluation and comparison:

1. Choose the alternative system which meets all or most of the set of mandatory requirements established for the new system to be developed.
2. Choose the alternative system which meets all or most of a set of desirable but not mandatory requirements for the new system.
3. Choose the alternative system which will cost the least to develop.
4. Choose the alternative system which will cost the least to operate on an annual basis after system installation.
5. Reject any alternative system whose annual operating costs, exclusive of developmental costs, exceed those of the present system.

Such rules, once established, are relatively easy to use because they can provide a quantitative means of evaluating the alternative systems. Qualitative or subjective decision rules might be easy to establish but very difficult to apply. For example, a decision to choose the alternative system which will provide a maximum amount of prestige to the library will be very difficult to apply because such a subjective criterion will be impossible to measure either before or after a system is installed and is operating.

A draft set of decision rules for selecting the best system can be prepared, then circulated widely among the staff and others for their comments and suggestions. Ideas and advice received should be incorporated into a revised draft for the project advisory committee to discuss and refine. It might be necessary to prepare several drafts before a satisfactory set of rules is acceptable to all. The final working set of decision rules should have the approval of the advisory committee before the process continues.

THE LIST OF ALTERNATIVES TO BE CONSIDERED

Once decision rules for selecting the best system have been established, a list of the alternative systems to be considered for possible development must be prepared. The various ways by which the library could possibly develop a new system should first be visualized or conceptualized. The library might, for example:

1. Purchase or lease a turnkey system.
2. Share a system with others through networking.
3. Adapt the system of another library for local use.
4. Develop a new system locally from scratch.

These methods of developing a computer-based library system are described more fully in chapter 1.

The actual systems to be considered next should be identified by asking colleagues, visiting exhibits at state, regional, or national conferences, scanning promotional literature sent to libraries, and reading articles, reports, and advertisements in the professional literature. The list might include, for example:

1. Three turnkey systems.
2. Two systems which can be shared through networking.
3. One system in another library which could be adapted.
4. A system to be developed locally from scratch.

The list can be circulated among the staff for their suggestions and comments, and the project advisory committee should discuss, revise, then approve the list. Other systems can be added at this time or later as the evaluation of the alternatives progresses.

COMPARISON OF ALTERNATIVES TO REQUIREMENTS

The alternative systems identified for consideration next should be examined with the purpose of determining which do and do not meet the requirements established by the library. It should be emphasized that the systems are to be compared to the library's requirements for a new system, and *not* to each other.

A chart facilitates the collection of data during the comparison (see Chart G-1 of Appendix G). The names of the alternative systems to be considered are listed along the top of the chart, and the library's requirements established earlier, along the left side. The features of each alternative system now are examined and compared to the set of requirements. A "yes" or "Y" is entered in the chart under the system's name and opposite the requirement being considered if the system does meet the specification, and "no" or "N" if it does not. If necessary, brief explanatory notes can be added in footnotes.

Information for determining whether an alternative system being considered does or does not meet specific requirements can be difficult to obtain. Vendor or network representatives usually are the best sources of information about systems being evaluated and compared. The representatives can provide descriptive brochures and other information about their products and possibly can demonstrate their systems in the library or at exhibits at professional conferences and meetings. When judging this information, the librarian must learn to separate *actual* from *planned* features of a system. Often, a representative presents a system as if some features are an actuality, whereas in truth they may not be available for many years to come. If in doubt, the librarian should ask the representative for the names of libraries in which the system with the questionable features are operable, then call or visit those libraries and ask for verification.

The staff of a data processing or computer center serving the library's host institution can be very helpful in providing and interpreting information about computers and computer-based systems, but not necessarily about computer-based *library* systems. Most centers have files of descriptive information about general computer hardware and software, and the library staff possibly can examine some or all of the equipment that might be used in support of a new system. Also, the project manager and other staff members can visit libraries where computer-based systems under consideration are already in operation.

The project advisory committee can scan the data collection chart after all alternative systems have been evaluated to determine those systems which do and do not meet the requirements. A list of a half dozen systems which meet all the requirements is a good working number for the economic comparisons to follow. If no system meets all the mandatory requirements, the list of specifications should be reviewed to determine if they are perhaps too stringent or unrealistic. If too many systems meet all the requirements, then the list is either too general or not exhaustive enough. It is not uncommon for a list of system requirements and the screening chart to be reviewed and revised several times before the process yields satisfactory results.

COMPARISON OF DEVELOPMENTAL COSTS

The one-time expenses necessary to start up each alternative system being considered can be estimated. These developmental costs, which are not expected to be repeated once an implemented system is operational, include design, hardware, application software, system software, site preparation, file conversion, staff training, other capital equipment, and miscellaneous expenses. Some costs might be the same for all or several systems being evaluated and compared. For example, file conversion or staff training might be the same for all.

A simple work chart can be prepared to collect the developmental costs for each system being considered. The detailed elements of developmental costs are listed along the left side, and the amounts estimated are shown beside the items in a separate column. All developmental costs are totaled and indicated at the bottom of the column. Another chart can be prepared to summarize the developmental costs for all the systems being considered (see Chart G-2 of Appendix G). The names of the systems are listed along the top of the chart, and the categories of developmental costs are listed along the left side. Data from the individual data collection forms are transferred to this summary chart.

Vendor and network representatives and the staff of a data processing or computer center serving the library's host institution again can serve as sources of information for developmental costs of the alternative systems being considered. Some costs gathered may be rough estimates, for exact data cannot be obtained until quotations are solicited from vendors during hardware and software acquisition (chapter 6) or until more developmental work is done. The analyst must proceed in the system comparison process with the best cost estimates available at the time. However, it must be realized that the study will be only as good as the cost estimates made for the individual systems.

At least 9 types of developmental costs must be estimated for each system being evaluated and compared:

- Design costs.
- Hardware costs.
- Application software costs.
- System software costs.
- Site preparation costs.
- File conversion costs.
- Staff training costs.
- Other capital costs.
- Miscellaneous costs.

Design Costs. Design costs, which must be estimated for those systems being considered to be developed locally from scratch or adapted from other libraries, include those expenses necessary to translate the library's requirements into a detailed plan or set of specifications for a new system. Costs of this creative process, in which a completely new scheme for handling work in the library is devised, usually include salaries and wages of systems analysts, consultants, and other staff who will plan and design a system; travel for visits to installations of computer-based systems, if necessary; supplies such as flowcharting templates, flowcharting forms, and specification binders; and miscellaneous expenses such as reproduction services necessary for design documentation. Design costs for turnkey systems and systems shared with others through networking will be included in the purchase or lease price of system software or the costs of transaction or service fees, and should not be considered in this activity. Additional information about system design can be found in chapter 5.

Hardware Costs. Hardware costs include the purchase of all hardware, such as a computer, magnetic disk drives, disk packs, magnetic tape units, printers, modems, visual display terminals, scanning wands, and other electronic and electromechanical devices necessary for a system. If hardware for a system is to be leased rather than purchased, the costs are considered annual operating costs and are not included in developmental costs. Additional information about hardware can be found in chapter 6.

Application Software Costs. Application software costs are the expenses necessary to design, code, test, debug, retest, and document the computer programs for a system. Such costs for a turnkey system are included as a package. However, for a system which is to be developed locally from scratch or to be adapted from another library, separate items must be estimated for salaries and wages of the systems analysts, programmers, and other staff who will prepare the application software; the computer time necessary to compile, debug, and test the programs; supplies such as coding forms and paper for the computer tests and documentation; and miscellaneous expenses such as reproduction costs necessary for software documentation.

The application software costs for a system shared through networking need not be considered because they will not be borne directly by the library. If the software for a turnkey system is to be leased rather than purchased, the costs are considered an annual operating expense and are not included in developmental costs.

System Software Costs. System software expenses can include the purchase of an operating system, compilers, and/or utility program for a computer system. Care should be taken to make certain that this type of software is not included in the purchase price of computer system hardware. If a computer is to be leased, its system software usually is also leased and therefore is considered an annual operating expense rather than a developmental one.

Site Preparation Costs. Site preparation costs might be necessary to modify the library building; install electrical circuits, plugs, and cables; and make alterations to or install heating, air conditioning, and humidity control systems prior to installation of a new system. The costs of dismantling, reassembling, and modifying furniture such as shelving also can be included. The estimates should include all labor and materials necessary to prepare a site. Additional information about site preparation can be found in chapter 7.

File Conversion Costs. Most computer-based systems require that one or more files be in a machine-readable form before it can operate. File conversion costs include the salaries and wages of staff who will edit, convert, check, and correct records; costs for hardware such as computer time and lease or purchase of keypunches or visual display terminals used to convert the files; and supplies such as punch cards or magnetic tape. If the library will have its files converted by an outside firm or organization, the costs usually are based on a per record conversion fee. Costs of converting files on a day-to-day basis after a system is implemented are considered annual operating expenses and are not included in developmental costs. Additional information about file conversion can be found in chapter 7.

Staff Training Costs. Training costs may be included as part of a software package by some turnkey system vendors, while others charge separately. If not provided by a vendor, a network operations office, or a local data processing or computer center, staff training must be supplied by the project manager, another member of the library staff, or a consultant. The expenses of providing the training by any of these methods should also be estimated. Additional information about staff training can be found in chapter 7.

Other Capital Costs. Capital costs other than for computer hardware can include any furniture or equipment necessary to operate a system, such as tables on which to place visual display terminals and storage cabinets and racks for magnetic tape and magnetic disk packs.

Miscellaneous Costs. Miscellaneous developmental expenses can include costs of shipping and installing the hardware, software, and other capital furniture and equipment, if not already included in other estimates such as hardware purchases, and costs of adding bar code or OCR labels to materials before a circulation system is installed. In this latter case, salaries and wages of the staff who will prepare and apply the labels and the costs of the necessary supplies must be estimated. Costs of adding bar codes or OCR labels to materials after system implementation is an annual operating expense and should not be included in this activity.

COMPARISON OF OPERATING COSTS

While developmental costs are not expected to be repeated once a system has been implemented and is operational, other costs will be repeated year after year for the lifetime of a system. Operating costs for each alternative system being considered can next be estimated. Those costs necessary to operate the existing system should also be included as a benchmark.

A separate chart should be prepared to collect and record the operating costs for each alternative system being considered. The individual years of the lifespan to be used in the study are listed along the top of the chart, and the cost elements to be considered, along the left side. As the costs are estimated for a system, the expenses are entered into the chart under the year and opposite the specific cost element. If a cost is not applicable for a system, "N/A" for "not applicable" or "$0.00" can be entered. Footnotes can be added if necessary. All operating costs for each year are totaled and included at the bottom of the columns. The operating costs can be summarized for all the alternatives being considered into one chart (see Chart G-3 of Appendix G). The names of the systems are listed along the top of the chart, and the categories of operating costs are listed along the left side. Data from the individual data collection forms are transferred to this summary chart.

Annual operating costs must be estimated for each year of the expected lifespan of each alternative system being evaluated. Therefore, the lifespan to be used must be determined before the estimates of operating expenses are made. The lifespan of a system usually is considered to be 5, 7, or 10 years, but any reasonable number can be selected as long as it is the same for all systems. A minimum lifespan would seem to be 5 years. Inflation can be built into the operating costs for each year of the lifespan, or inflation can be ignored for the purposes of this study on the assumption that the increases would be the same for each alternative system being considered and therefore would not bias one system over another as long as all are treated the same.

Reliable sources of information on which to base estimates of operating costs for the alternative systems being considered must be identified. Vendors of turnkey systems and hardware in general, network representatives, and the staff of a computer center in the library's host institution again are the primary sources of operating cost information. Several looseleaf reference services include cost information for computer systems of all sizes and for software, data communications, and other peripheral devices. (See the bibliography of this book for citations.) These services are too expensive for small libraries, but they should be available for use in other libraries or in a nearby computer center.

Operating costs, which usually are computed on an annual basis, include:

- Salaries and wages.
- Supplies.

- Hardware leases.
- Hardware maintenance.
- Software maintenance.
- Transaction and service fees.
- Miscellaneous costs.

Costs of space rental, buildings and grounds maintenance, heating and air conditioning, telephone services, staff travel to professional meetings, continuing education, and similar expenses usually are not considered in this type of study, on the assumption that they would be the same for any system which might be installed. However, if desired, these costs can be computed and included in the estimates.

Salaries and Wages. Salaries and wages include the costs for all staff, both full- and part-time, required to manage and operate each system being considered, estimated for each year of the lifespan selected. If desired, fringe benefits can also be included.

Supply Costs. In addition to the usual paper, pens, paper clips, typewriter ribbons, and other office supplies, supply costs also are estimated for such items as customized forms, catalog cards, magnetic tapes, bar code or OCR labels, and other specialized consumables necessary to operate a system each year of its projected life.

Hardware Lease Costs. Hardware lease costs include expenses for the lease of any hardware such as a computer, magnetic disk drives, magnetic tape units, printers, modems, visual display terminals, scanning wands, and other electronic and electromechanical devices necessary for a system. The leases must be estimated for each year of the lifespan period. If hardware is to be purchased rather than leased, the costs are considered developmental and are not included in this activity. Additional information about hardware can be found in chapter 6.

Software Lease Costs. If application and system software are to be leased rather than purchased or prepared locally, these costs must be estimated for each year of the projected lifespan of a system. Software lease costs for systems shared through networking are not borne directly by the library and can be ignored in this study. The 2 types of software should be listed in the data collection chart separately. If software is to be purchased rather than leased, the costs are considered developmental and are not included as operating costs. Additional information about software can be found in chapters 5 and 6.

Hardware Maintenance Costs. Hardware must be maintained after a system has been installed, whether the equipment is to be purchased or leased. Contracts must be made with the vendors or other firms to keep the hardware in good operating condition. These costs will be necessary for each year of the projected lifespan period for all hardware required by each system. The annual maintenance can be estimated at roughly 1 percent per month of the original purchase value of the hardware. For example, if a visual display terminal is valued at $2,500, then its maintenance costs each year would be approximately $300 ($2,500 × 1 percent × 12 months). Additional information about hardware maintenance can be found in chapter 6.

Software Maintenance Costs. Software, like hardware, must be maintained in good operating condition, and these maintenance costs will be necessary for each year of the projected lifetime of each system. Changes must be made to correct errors and update programs in general when necessary. Both application and system software, whether purchased or leased, require regular maintenance. Contracts can be made with the vendor, other firms, or the data processing or computer center serving the library's host institution to maintain the software for a system, depending upon the system. Software maintenance for systems shared through networking is provided by the network organization and thus need not be considered in this study. The software maintenance contract also can be estimated at roughly 1 percent per month of the original purchase value of the software. For example, if a software package is valued at $15,000, then its annual maintenance cost each year would be approximately $1,800 ($15,000 × 1 percent × 12 months).

Transaction or Service Fees. Systems shared through networking usually require fees charged to the library for each transaction completed in the system. For example, OCLC, Inc. charges a fee each time a record in its database is used to prepare a set of catalog cards. These costs, if applicable, must be estimated for each year of the projected lifetime of a system.

Miscellaneous Costs. Any miscellaneous costs for a system must be estimated for each year of the lifetime span. Some examples of miscellaneous costs include purchase of catalog card sets, leases of extra telephones for remote terminals, and energy to power a special air-conditioning unit required for a computer. If desired, any or all of these can be treated as a separate cost element in the chart rather than grouped together as a miscellaneous cost.

SELECTION OF THE BEST SYSTEM

Once all comparisons have been made, the results can be analyzed and summarized and the best system selected, using the decision rules for selecting the best system as established at the beginning of this phase.

The operating costs estimated for the alternative systems being considered can be analyzed and summarized to facilitate their comparison and evaluation. For example, the cumulative costs for operating each system over the lifespan period can be computed by summing the operating costs for all the individual years. In such a case, if the annual operating costs for the 5 years of a system's lifetime are, respectively, $50,000, $52,000, $54,000, $56,000, and $58,000, then the cumulative operating costs for that system are:

$$\$50,000 + 52,000 + 54,000 + 56,000 + 58,000$$

or $270,000 for the 5 years.

The average annual operating costs for each system's lifespan then can be obtained by using the following formula:

$$\text{Average Annual Cost for a System} = \frac{\text{Cumulative Operating Costs for a System's Lifespan}}{\text{Number of Years in the Lifespan}}$$

For example, if the cumulative operating costs for a system are $270,000, then the average operating costs for a 5-year lifespan would be:

$$\frac{\$270,000}{5} \quad \text{or} \quad \$54,000.$$

The average monthly operating costs for each system then can be obtained by using the following formula:

$$\text{Average Monthly Cost for a System} = \frac{\text{Average Annual Operating Cost for a System}}{12 \text{ months}}$$

For example, if the average annual costs of operating a system is $54,000, then the average monthly operating costs will be:

$$\frac{\$54,000}{12} \quad \text{or} \quad \$4,500.$$

The results of these and other evaluations completed in this phase can be transferred into a decision chart which can facilitate and document the decision-making process when the best system is selected. The names of the systems evaluated during the study are listed along the left side of the chart, and headings such as "meets all mandatory requirements," "meets all desirable requirements," "developmental costs," "cumulative annual operating costs," "average annual operating costs," and "average monthly operating costs" can be placed along the top (see Chart G-4 of Appendix G). Whether or not each system considered met the library's requirements is indicated by either "Yes" or "No" opposite the name of the system.

The estimated developmental and operating costs and their analyses are entered as dollar amounts in the chart opposite the names of the respective systems. Footnotes can be added to the chart if necessary. A scan down the chart then quickly indicates which system will be best for development by the library, based upon the comparison and estimates made during the study of the identified alternatives and the comparison of the results against the predetermined decision rules.

DOCUMENTATION OF THE RESULTS

Once alternative systems have been evaluated and compared and the best selected, the results can be documented for approval by the library director, governing and funding authorities, and others. A report documenting the study should include as a minimum:

1. The objective or purpose of the study.
2. A brief overview describing the method used to complete the study.
3. The decision rules established for selecting the best system.
4. The list of requirements established for the new system.
5. A list of the alternatives considered, with a brief description of each.
6. The chart resulting from the comparison of the alternatives to the library's requirements.
7. The chart summarizing the estimated developmental costs for the remaining alternatives.
8. The chart analyzing and summarizing the estimated operating costs for the remaining alternatives.
9. The decision chart on which the selection of the best system was based.
10. A brief description of the system determined to be the best.

Narrative introductions to each item can be included. The report can be presented to the project advisory committee and library director and to the city manager, mayor, president, board, council, or other group advising or governing the library for their authorization or approval to proceed with the project. A sample report of a system evaluation and comparison can be found in Appendix G.

Chapter 5
Detailed Design Specifications

The preparation of detailed design specifications is essential in developing a computer-based library system, particularly one which is being developed locally from scratch. As the "blueprint" for the new system, design specifications are used by programmers or coders to prepare the sets of instructions which the computer follows in processing information in the system.

Specifically, this chapter includes discussions of:

- The modular approach.
- Input and output specifications.
- Processing specifications.
- Data base specifications.
- Other design specifications.
- Design documentation.

THE MODULAR APPROACH

The library system to be designed can be divided into a number of smaller subsystems to facilitate the design process. This systems approach provides a method of segmenting a large complex system into a number of smaller, less complex components which can be more readily visualized and analyzed as specifications are prepared. However, while each part is designed separately to operate independently of all others, the subsystems are interrelated and interacting and, therefore, can not be considered in isolation from each other. Each must be designed to operate effectively and efficiently in consort with all others.

The system to be designed should be separated into at least 2 levels of subsystems (Figure 5-1). Some designers prefer to identify the major subsystems first, then divide each into functional parts, while others prefer to identify functional subsystems first, then arrange related functions together into broader logical groupings or subsystems. Each approach is correct, and the end results are the same. As the design process continues, subsystems can be redefined and functions can be combined, divided, or moved to other subsystems.

Figure 5-1. The levels of subsystems useful during system design.

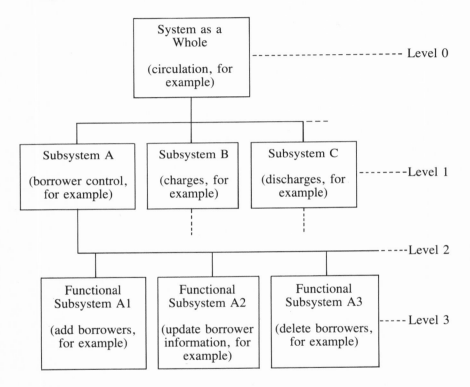

Each large system of the library consists of a number of major subsystems, as depicted in Figures 1-1 and 5-1. These should be identified and defined for the system to be designed. Each large subsystem represents a broad functional area of a system and is used primarily for organizational and administrative purposes. For example, a circulation system might contain component borrower control, checkout, discharge, renewal, reserve, overdues, and fines subsystems; an acquisitions system might contain searching and verification, order preparation, receiving and canceling, and fund accounting subsystems; a cataloging system might contain cataloging with copy, original cataloging, and data base maintenance subsystems; and a binding system might contain commercial binding, commercial rebinding, in-house binding, and in-house mending and repair subsystems. A minimum of 2 subsystems must be identified.

Each major subsystem identified should have its own reason for being, with a goals statement specifying the contributions of the subsystem to the overall mission of the system as a whole. For example, the goal of a borrower control subsystem might be simply to record, store, and maintain pertinent and correct information about each borrower eligible to borrow library materials, and the goal of an order preparation subsystem might be to transfer bibliographic and other acquisition information onto forms which can be forwarded to vendors as purchase orders for materials. Subsystem goals statements must neither contradict the overriding mission of the system as a whole nor overlap the missions of other subsystems.

The functional subsystems comprising each major subsystem next must be identified and defined. A functional subsystem is the smallest component of a system which can be designed separately to operate independently of all others; the work of a system is performed on this level. Many or all of these may already have been identified during system evaluation and comparison in chapter 4. A goals statement can also be prepared for each of the functions, which must contradict neither the overriding mission of the system as a whole nor of other subsystems.

INPUT AND OUTPUT SPECIFICATIONS

The input and output for each functional subsystem must be identified, defined, and described. The result will be a set of input and output specifications for the system being designed.

Identification of Input and Output of Functional Subsystems. The input and output expected of each functional subsystem to be designed must be identified. The output, which is the end result or product of a function, should be identified first. The output could be:

1. Records which have been created or completed.
2. Transactions which have been completed.
3. Lists or reports which have been compiled or produced.
4. Visual displays of information which has been processed in some manner or retrieved from a file.
5. Materials which have been processed in some manner.

Working backwards, the input required to produce the desired output then can be identified. The input can be:

1. Forms which will be filled out or completed.
2. A specific amount or measure of predefined information which will be processed in some manner into an output.
3. Library materials which will be processed in some manner into a finished output.

For example, the input and output of some subsystems might be as follows:

Borrower Registration Subsystem

  Input: Blank registration forms, blank identification cards, and predefined information about borrowers to be registered.

  Output: Borrower registration records and identification cards ready to use.

Charge or Checkout Subsystem

  Input: Blank circulation charge forms, date-due forms, and predefined information about a transaction which will transpire.

  Output: Circulation transaction records and completed date-due forms.

Order Preparation Subsystem

  Input: Blank purchase order forms or multiple-copy order forms and predefined bibliographic and ordering information about each title to be ordered.

  Output: Purchase orders, processing file records, and accounting system entry records.

The amount of input and output for each subsystem should be kept to a minimum to reduce waste and avoid providing information that will never be used. Each subsystem must have at least one output; some might require only one output, while others might have several. Sometimes the distinction between intput and output is hazy, particularly when the only difference between them is a conditional change: that is, when input is unprocessed information and output is processed information. In most cases, the output of one function becomes the input into another.

Purposes of Input and Output. Once the input and output of each functional subsystem have been identified, their purposes should be defined. Some input and output may have only one purpose, while others may have several; each must have at least one reason for existing. For example, the purpose of a purchase order might be:

> To provide a list of items the library wishes to purchase, including sufficient information to enable the vendor to identify and ship the materials wanted. In addition, the vendor must be given clear but brief shipping and billing instructions.

Or the purpose of an order card might be:

> To provide a means by which faculty and staff can request the purchase of materials, record the results of verification, searching, and collecting bibliographic and ordering information pertaining to the request for purchase, serve as a source document for entry of data into the online system, and serve as a temporary backup record in case the online record is lost or destroyed.

General Specifications for Input and Output. General specifications for each input and output should be prepared. These specifications supply a narrative description of each, including its format and size. For example, general specifications for a purchase order might be as follows:

> The purchase order is 8½ inches in size, printed on a 2-part, carbon-interleaved form. The items printed on its face are heading description, shipping and billing instructions, identifying words over the columns, and a signature line.

Or the general specifications for output from a file search might be:

> The information resulting from file searches are to be displayed on a CRT screen of 24 lines vertical and 80 characters horizontal. The data elements are preceded by protected field tags of highlighted intensity. Prompts for possible actions by the operator are displayed on the bottom line of the screen.

Or the general specifications for an order card might be:

> The order card is 3 by 5 inches in size, on light index card stock. The items preprinted on the form are brief instructions for its completion and routing and data field tags and blanks for brief bibliographic and ordering information.

Input and Output Data Requirements. The data or information required by each input and output should be identified and described. The following should be specified for each data element required:

1. Name or description of the data element.
2. The length of the data (that is, whether the data are variable or fixed in length and the expected maximum length).
3. Whether the data are alphabetic, numeric, or alphanumeric.

For example, data requirements for an overdue notice might be specified as follows:

Data Element	Length	Type
Date of notice	12 characters fixed	Alphanumeric
Classification number	Variable up to 25 characters	Alphanumeric
Brief title	Variable up to 30 characters	Alphanumeric
Due date	12 characters fixed	Alphanumeric
Library branch name	10 characters fixed	Alphanumeric
Borrower's name	Variable up to 50 characters	Alphanumeric
Borrower's address	Variable up to 50 characters	Alphanumeric
Borrower's ID number	9 characters fixed	Numeric

There should be a good balance between the amount of information provided and that which is actually needed by the anticipated user of the input or output. Information which will never or seldom be referred to by a system user, for example, should not be included on an output. It is mainly a matter of judgment as to whether the designer is providing too much or too little information.

Preliminary Layouts for Input and Output. A tentative sketch or layout should be prepared for each form, report, or visual display used as input or output. Forms should not be duplicated or printed at this time, because they may be changed during the programming and testing activities. The layouts should be completed and a supply of forms prepared during the implementation phase (chapter 7). Some general guidelines for input and output layout include the following:

1. Try to make each form, report, or visual display serve as many functions as possible.
2. Design the input and output to serve the human users of the system, rather than the machines.
3. Use a box design if possible, with columns or rows and individual elements of data adequately and clearly identified. If possible, do not use abbreviations that are undecipherable.

4. Provide the minimum amount of data or information to achieve a desired result.
5. Group related information together for ease of locating and using the information.
6. Attempt to design forms, reports, and visual displays with an uncluttered, easy-to-read format. Do not put data or characters so close together that distinguishing displayed elements apart is difficult or impossible.
7. Provide a means of emphasizing or highlighting important data or information.
8. Use standard dimensions for forms and reports in order to minimize costs.

While some preprinted forms are essential, many output reports may be printed on blank paper because, in most computer-based systems, the output data are formatted inside the machine before a report is actually printed.

Frequency and Number of Input and Output. Finally, the frequency and number of each input and output should be specified. The frequency indicates how many times during a day, week, month, or year the output will be produced, and the number indicates the input and output count required each time the output is produced. The chart in Figure 5-2 shows how the frequency and number of input and output for a subsystem can be specified and summarized.

Figure 5-2. A chart depicting the frequency and number of input and output for a system.

Input/Output	Frequency Produced or Used	Estimated Number per Year (or Week or Month)
Borrower registration forms	Daily	15,000
Borrower identification cards	Daily	15,000
First overdue notices	Daily	53,500
Second overdue notices	Daily	42,000
Third overdue notices	Daily	35,200
Fines notices	Daily	35,500
List of delinquent borrowers	Monthly	12
Circulation statistics	Monthly	12
Borrower records displays	Daily	490,000
Circulation transactions	Daily	350,000

PROCESSING SPECIFICATIONS

Processing specifications must be prepared for each functional subsystem of the system being designed. The workflow—the movement of information, materials, and other objects from operation to operation through a function or from function to function—for each must also be established. Some designers prepare processing specifications before preparing input and output specifications, while others prefer the reverse. Others establish a general workflow through all functions of a subsystem, followed by preparation of its input and output specifications. Still others prefer to work on input and output specifications and workflow simultaneously.

Every functional subsystem of a library system has a set or group of specified and predefined processing operations which are performed on the input of information, library materials, and other physical objects to achieve the desired end result or output. The input is converted to output as these step-by-step tasks are performed in an orderly, specified sequence.

The designer should assemble, organize, and review the specifications previously prepared for each functional subsystem before beginning to prepare the processing specifications. Continual reference to this documentation is necessary as preparation of requirements proceeds and the various methods of processing input into output are analyzed and compared.

Decision Flowcharts. Detailed flowcharts should be prepared to depict the workflow for each functional subsystem. By graphically or pictorially representing the sequence of operations performed on information, materials, and other physical objects moving through a function, flowcharts are useful as:

1. Aids in visualizing the workflow as the processing operations are designed.
2. Parts of system documentation. The charts provide a snapshot of the system and become the standard for operation of the system after its implementation.
3. General communications devices for teaching and training others how the system will operate. Since flowcharts are widely used and understood, they are a medium of communications between the designer and others who wish to understand the system.

There are several types or families of flowcharts, including system, procedure, logic or decision, process, forms, and layout charts. The designer can use one, several, or all of these types during the development phase of a library system, depending upon personal preference or upon the peculiar qualities of a particular type of chart. Logic or decision flowcharts are described here because they are most often used in systems design and are the simplest to learn and apply. These charts depict in detailed form the specific operations performed in a function on input to produce output. They specify all decisions which are to be made in the flow of work and the alternative courses of action to be taken as a result of these decisions.

Decision flowcharts are constructed by stringing together symbols or boxes of varying shapes representing operations or processes, decisions, storage, and other activities. Short, concise descriptions and explanations are placed inside the symbols. Standardized symbols have been accepted by both the American National Standards Institute (ANSI) and the International Standards Organization (ISO). Over 30 symbols are available, grouped into 4 basic categories:

- Basic symbols.
- Input/Output symbols.
- Equipment symbols.
- Special process symbols.

Only a handful of symbols are essential in most cases, especially for beginners. The symbols useful to the beginner are shown in Figure 5-3.

Flowlines are used to connect the symbols in a chart, with arrowheads pointing the direction of the flow of work. The normal sequence of a flowchart is from the top of a page downwards and from left to right, though a sequence from the left side of the page to the right is not uncommon. Each page of a set of charts should be fully identified and numbered. The connector symbol is used to guide the reader from one page of the set to another. When a decision is necessary during the processing flow, a decision block is inserted, with a ''yes'' line emerging from one point of the diamond and a ''no'' line from another; no other choices are usually possible. The processing flow is thus broken into 2 diverging sequences of steps indicating the processing steps resulting if either possible path is taken. Sample decision flowcharts can be found in Appendix H.

Narrative Descriptions to Accompany Flowcharts. A set of narrative descriptions or specifications for each block in the set of decision flowcharts for the functional subsystem must be prepared to accompany the charts. This is necessary to provide a more detailed description or explanation of the workflow than can be included in the charts themselves. Some designers prefer to begin development of a function's workflow with the narrative descriptions of the processes, then prepare the necessary flowcharts.

The narrative descriptions can be placed on the flowcharts on the same pages as their accompanying symbols, or each symbol in the charts can be numbered and the descriptions placed on separate sheets with corresponding numbers linking them to the charts.

Interfaces between Functional Subsystems. As a final step, the flow-charts for each functional subsystem should be checked for a smooth flow of work from one function to another. If bottlenecks, overlapping operations, or inefficiencies are located, then input, output, or operations must be redesigned.

Figure 5-3. The flowcharting symbols useful to the beginner.

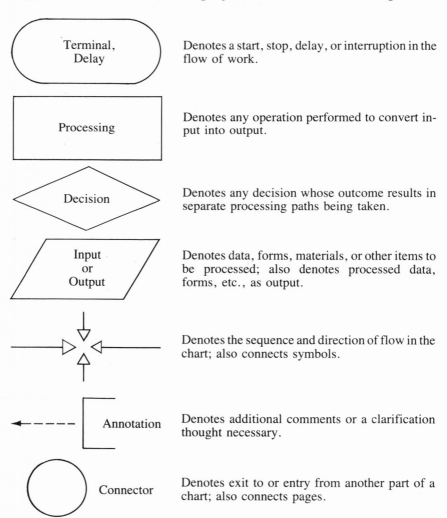

Terminal, Delay — Denotes a start, stop, delay, or interruption in the flow of work.

Processing — Denotes any operation performed to convert input into output.

Decision — Denotes any decision whose outcome results in separate processing paths being taken.

Input or Output — Denotes data, forms, materials, or other items to be processed; also denotes processed data, forms, etc., as output.

Denotes the sequence and direction of flow in the chart; also connects symbols.

Annotation — Denotes additional comments or a clarification thought necessary.

Connector — Denotes exit to or entry from another part of a chart; also connects pages.

DATA BASE SPECIFICATIONS

Specifications for the files or data base supporting the various subsystems of the system being developed must be prepared. To facilitate preparing files or data base specifications, the designer can prepare a data usage chart to summarize the data requirements already specified for the various inputs and outputs of the functional subsystems. The chart, which is simple, easy to construct, and easy to read, enables the designer to visualize the pool of data needed in all the functions as a whole, what data are common to several inputs and outputs, what data are missing, and what data might be eliminated, combined, or separated. The inputs and outputs of the system are listed along the top of the chart (Figure 5-4) and each data element along the left-hand side of the chart. An ''x'' is placed under each particular input or output in which a data element is used.

Figure 5-4. An information usage chart summarizing the forms, records, and reports and pieces of data contained in each for a system.

Data Element	Check-In Record	Bindery Slip	Serials Record	Card Catalog	Serials Printout	Order Card
Title	X	X	X	X	X	X
Frequency	X		X	X	X	X
Numbers per volume	X	X	X			
Date-due	X					
Dealer	X					
Fund	X					X
Publisher	X			X	X	X
Call number	X	X	X	X	X	
Binding color		X				
Height		X				
Copies	X		X		X	X
ISSN	X		X	X	X	X
Cost	X		X			X
Beginning date				X	X	X
Indexing terms				X	X	
Branch locations	X		X	X	X	X

General Requirements for the Data Base. The general requirements for the data base should be established; these requirements may already have been prepared during the system evaluation and comparison phase (chapter 4). For example, some general requirements for the data base supporting an acquisitions system might be that:

1. All files must be online at all times.
2. Online addition, deletion, and changes to all files must be possible.
3. MARC (machine-readable cataloging) tags must be retained for all bibliographic data.
4. The system must allow bibliographic records to be transferred electronically from the acquisitions subsystem to the cataloging subsystem, without manual reentry of data.

Identification and Description of Files. The designer must identify and describe the probable files required by the various functions of the system being designed, keeping in mind that during preparation of the computer programs some might be combined, divided, or changed. The data usage chart prepared above can be examined to determine what files might be necessary. The files identified can be listed along the top of a chart similar to that in Figure 5-4, and each data element to be included in the files, along the left-hand side of the chart. An "x" is placed under each file in which a data element is used. If desired, a similar chart also can be prepared for all data elements to summarize their characteristics, and another chart can be prepared to summarize the use of files by all functions. The functions are listed along the top of the chart, and the files along the left-hand side of the chart. An "x" is placed under each function in which a file is used.

OTHER DESIGN SPECIFICATIONS

Other design specifications may be necessary for a new system, such as:

1. Security specifications.
2. Audit control specifications.
3. Backup or recovery specifications.

Security Specifications. Specifications for security of information in data files and access to the use of the software and its functions can be specified. For example:

1. Only authorized staff can enter, alter, or delete information from the files.
2. A system of passwords must be provided to control access to the various functions.

Audit Control Specifications. Methods can be devised to trace the process of data from input through output or backwards from output to the original input. This can be necessary when tracing errors in computations or data and to meet financial audit requirements. For example:

1. The system must provide a listing of all errors encountered in processing data.
2. The system must provide check points throughout the processing of data.
3. All outdated records must be retained for a period of 2 years after they have been superceded or updated.

Backup or Recovery Specifications. Occasionally, records or entire files can be irretrievably lost through negligence, vandalism, sabotage, accident, or hardware or software failures. Methods of recovering or reconstructing lost data must be planned and provided for. For example:

1. A method of rapidly duplicating all files for backup purposes must be provided.
2. All transactions conducted in the system must be logged onto tape as magnetic disk files are updated.
3. A means of restoring files using a backup file supplied by a log tape of all transactions completed since the last backup run must be provided.

DESIGN DOCUMENTATION

Upon completion of the design phase, a design report is prepared and submitted for approval. Continuation of the project into the programming and testing activities usually is not permitted until the design has been accepted and approved. The results of all design work performed in this phase are reviewed for completeness and accuracy, and any incomplete or incorrect specifications are redone.

A draft design report can be prepared and circulated widely before it is formally submitted for approval. (Part of a sample design report is shown in Appendix H.) The report should include as a minimum:

1. Purpose of the report.
2. Background for the report.

3. System goals statement.
4. System environment.
5. System overview.
6. Design assumptions and constraints.
7. Detailed design specifications:
   a. General specifications.
   b. Input and output specifications.
   c. Processing flow specifications.
   d. Data base specifications.
   e. Other specifications.

Formal or informal meetings and discussions can be held to solicit input from others and gain their support for the design. Their comments and suggestions for improving the document should be evaluated carefully and, if possible, incorporated into the document before the final report is prepared. After the draft has circulated and suggestions and comments have been incorporated, the report to be submitted formally to library management and others is prepared. The report should be neatly typed according to the criteria of an acceptable guide for preparing papers or manuscripts. All illustrations such as flowcharts and layouts should be neatly and, if possible, professionally drawn. The report can be photocopied or reproduced by other methods, then placed into neatly labeled ring binders, stapled inside stiff covers, or bound in some other appropriate manner.

The design report should be submitted for approval to the project advisory committee, library management, and, if necessary, to the library's governing and/or funding authorities. After it has been approved by the project advisory committee and by the library director, the report can be presented to the city manager, mayor, president, board, council, or other group advising or governing the library for their authorization or approval to proceed with the project. Even if persons or groups have advisory powers only, their approval should be sought and obtained before work on the project continues. The report could be approved outright, rejected, or approved pending certain modifications to the design specifications.

Chapter 6
Acquisition of Hardware, Software, and Vendor Assistance

The purpose of this phase of a systems projects is to procure or acquire any hardware, software, hardware and software maintenance, and/or other vendor assistance essential to install and support a computer-based system being developed. A checklist of hardware, software, and items of vendor assistance for typical computer-based library systems is shown in Appendix I. Most libraries are required to acquire hardware, software, and vendor assistance through a bidding process or at least a process wherein proposals or quotations are solicited from a number of prospective vendors and the best or least expensive is selected for acquisition.

Specifically, this chapter includes discussions of:

- Request for proposal (RFP) development.
- Decision rules for selection of the best system.
- Solicitation of responses to an RFP.
- Validation of responses from vendors.
- Contract negotiation.

RFP DEVELOPMENT

Quotations, bids, or proposals can be solicited from hardware and/or software manufacturers or vendors using a request for information (RFI), request for quotation (RFQ), or request for proposal (RFP). The RFP is essential to:

1. Convey to prospective vendors the exact needs and requirements of the library for hardware, software, hardware maintenance, software maintenance, and/or other assistance.

2. Obtain exact information, quotations, bids, or proposals from several vendors who would like to supply the items to the library.
3. Provide a means of fairly and uniformly comparing and evaluating responses to the document from the several vendors.

The RFP is usually prepared through the combined efforts of the project manager, the project advisory committee, a project consultant, if any, the library's purchasing department, and perhaps the staff of a local data processing or computer center serving the library. Extreme care should be taken if a favored vendor is asked to assist in preparing the document; the RFP should reflect the true needs of the library rather than needs molded to fit a specific vendor's product. Also, it usually is in the best interests of the library to develop a document to which several vendors would have a reasonable chance of responding with good bids. Through competitive bidding, the library could gain better prices for hardware and software and retain a sense of fair play in the process. A set of closed specifications—that is, specifications written so that one and only one vendor can meet them—eliminates competitive bidding, stifles competition, could easily result in higher prices for a product or service, and is illegal in some situations.

Formats of RFPs vary from region to region and from institution to institution. Usually, an RFP consists of 4 basic parts or sections:

1. An introduction.
2. General ground rules for the RFP.
3. The library's requirements for the hardware, software, maintenance, and/or vendor assistance to be acquired.
4. Instructions to vendors for submitting responses to the RFP.

A typical document is described below, and a sample RFP is shown in Appendix J.

The Introduction to an RFP. The introduction to an RFP should include:

1. A statement of the purpose of the document.
2. Background information for prospective bidders.

The purpose of the RFP should be clearly but briefly stated. For example, the purpose might be stated in this manner:

The intent of this request for proposal (RFP) is to specify the requirements of the Valhalla Library for a minicomputer system, application software, and hardware and software maintenance to support its circulation and acquisitions systems.

Or:

> The purpose of this request for proposal (RFP) is to request bids (or quotations) from prospective vendors for an automated circulation system for the Valhalla Library.

Or:

> The purpose of this request is to procure equipment, software, and vendor support that will provide the Valhalla Library with a computer-based acquisitions and cataloging system.

Because most if not all vendors who potentially might wish to respond to an RFP will not be familiar with the library, some background information should be provided to give them a brief overview of how the hardware and/or software will be used. Brief descriptions of the following might be included:

1. The library and its history and setting or environment.
2. The existing system.
3. How the proposed equipment and/or software will be used or how the new system will operate.

General Ground Rules for an RFP. The general guidelines or ground rules concerning contacts and negotiations with prospective vendors and the handling of quotations, bids, or proposals from vendors should be defined and described. The following can be included as ground rules:

1. *Contact Person(s).* The name, title, mailing address, and telephone number should be listed for the person(s) who can be contacted by vendors for additional information or for clarification of information about the RFP. The library may, for legal or documentation purposes, require that all inquiries about the RFP be in writing and submitted by a specific date.
2. *A Timetable.* A timetable of dates and times pertinent to the RFP should be specified. The following might be included:
   a. Last date and time for receiving inquiries about the RFP.
   b. Last date and time the library will accept requests for briefings, interviews, or demonstrations from vendors.
   c. Date and time when quotations, bids, or proposals are due.
   d. Date and time the responses will be opened.
   e. Time period for demonstrations of vendors' equipment and/or software.
   f. Date the contract will be awarded.
   g. Date the library expects delivery or installation of equipment and/or software.

3. *Delivery of Bids.* The number of copies of responses to be submitted by vendors and the name and address of the person to receive the documents should be clearly specified.
4. *Demonstrations.* The library may require a demonstration to determine the ability of hardware and/or software to perform as specified by vendors. Details outlining how the demonstrations will be conducted should be included in the RFP. Usually, dates for demonstrations are negotiated with vendors after proposal evaluations.
5. *Contractual Expectations.* General information about contractual provisions, such as general contractual terms, contract changes, performance bonds, delivery times, and penalty clauses for late or no delivery should be clearly specified.
6. *Method of Cost Proposal Wanted.* The library should stipulate how it wishes cost information to be presented by vendors for equipment, software, and other services. For example, the library can request vendors to supply outright purchase prices, prices for leasing or renting, or prices for lease-purchase of items. The library might wish to stipulate that it be able to pay an amount down and a specified method of financing the balance over a period of years or months. Forms to be completed by vendors for cost information can be included in this section or as an appendix to the RFP. The library should include a proviso that all costs bid be firm for a specified period of time.
7. *Evaluation of Proposals or Bids.* How bids or proposals will be evaluated can be briefly described, and the evaluation criteria can be delineated, if desired. For example:

> Proposals, bids, or quotations will be evaluated by a team of librarians and data processing specialists, who will select the proposal offering the best and lowest bid [or quotation] conforming to its specifications.

Hardware Requirements. Detailed requirements can be prepared and included in an RFP for hardware to be acquired. By this time, the project manager should have a good idea of the hardware required to implement the system being developed. If not, all previous phases of the project should be reviewed; the data processing staff in the computer center serving the library or the project consultant, if one, should be consulted; and the specific items which must be acquired should be identified. For example, for a turnkey system the library might need to acquire the following hardware:

1. A central processing unit (CPU) and cabinet.
2. A magnetic tape drive and controller.

3. One or more magnetic disk drives and controller(s).
4. Operator's console.
5. Line or serial printer(s).
6. Data communications control device(s).
7. Data communications modem(s).
8. CRT terminals.
9. OCR or bar code scanner(s) and controller(s).
10. Essential cabling for the system.

For shared or locally developed systems, some or all of these items may need to be acquired, depending upon the hardware already available to the library. For example, to implement a system shared with others through networking, the library might need to acquire only CRT or typewriter terminals and some equipment to control the data communications channels into the library.

The requirements for hardware are similar to those prepared in chapter 3; in fact, many of the requirements can be copied directly from activities completed during the early phases of the project. These detailed requirements should be prepared for each type or piece of hardware to be acquired. Size, speed, functional characteristics, noise level, heat generation, expandability, flexibility, reliability, and performance should be specified, when applicable. Each requirement should be considered either *mandatory* or *desirable*; separate listings of each can be made if desired.

The staff of the library's data processing or computer center or a consultant can be very helpful in development of hardware requirements. For example, the following are some actual requirements for hardware used by various libraries:

1. The CPU must have a minimum internal memory size of 128K bytes.
2. The CPU's internal memory must be expandable to a minimum of 256K bytes.
3. The magnetic disk drives must provide a minimum of 1.75 times the storage required for the library's data files described in Table X.
4. The printer must have 132 alphanumeric print positions, with a minimum printing speed of 200 lines per minute of alphanumeric information, using a standard ASCII character set.
5. The CRT visual display terminals must have a minimum screen capacity of 1,920 characters of 24 lines vertically and 80 characters horizontally on each line.
6. The CRT terminals must have a usable screen of at least 12 inches diagonal measurement.

7. The CRT terminals must have audible alarms.
8. The CRT terminals must be RS-232C compatible with CPU above.
9. The CRT terminals must operate at standard data transmission rates from 300 to 9600 baud.
10. The optical scanners must be capable of interfacing (hardwired) with the above CRT display terminals.

System Software Requirements. Detailed requirements can be prepared and included in an RFP for system software—such as an operating system, programming languages, data base management system, or utility programs—to be acquired. Functional characteristics, reliability, expandability, flexibility, and performance should also be specified for system software. Each system requirement should be labeled either as mandatory or as desirable.

The staff of the library's data processing or computer center or a consultant again can be very helpful in developing these specifications. The following are some sample requirements for system software specified by various libraries in their RFPs:

1. The operating system must provide for automatic loading of programs into internal memory from the program library.
2. The operating system must include standard error-handling routines to minimize operator intervention.
3. The operating system must enable a minimum of one batch program to be executed in the background while other programs are being executed in the foreground.
4. The operating system must be adjustable to the addition of future peripheral equipment with only minor software changes.
5. A COBOL compiler based on the 1974 American National Standards Institute standards must be provided.
6. The COBOL compiler must include debugging routines for snapshot dumps and complete diagnostics.
7. A sort/merge utility system must be provided which will support multidisk files, incorporate user-written processing before and after the sorting/merging process, and use either disk or tape input and output.
8. A text editor must be provided which can handle files with various record formats and use either tape or disk as input and output.
9. A set of housekeeping routines must be provided which can copy programs or files to any output device, display or delete files, and reorganize files.

10. A set of file conversion routines must be provided which can perform tape-to-disk and disk-to-tape conversion and duplicate or copy one disk file to another.

<u>Application Software Requirements</u>. Detailed functional requirements can be prepared and included for application software to be acquired in the RFP. Requirements should be included for each subsystem of the system, with a separate general set of specifications. For example, the following are some actual requirements for the application software of a circulation system used by various libraries.

General System Requirements

1. The system must not require a high level of data processing or computer knowledge or training by the library staff.
2. The files in auxiliary storage must be protected from accidental erasure by the library staff.
3. The system must be expandable to accommodate twice the library's current circulation load without redesign of software or replacement of hardware.
4. A system of passwords must be provided limiting access to each program to authorized library staff only.

Borrower Control Subsystem Requirements

1. The library staff must be able to add, delete, or change borrower information in the system's files.
2. The system must provide for the following data elements for each borrower: borrower identification number; borrower's full name, address, and telephone number; and one field for free-form data.
3. The system must accept borrower identification numbers in OCR (or bar code) format, while also providing for manual keyboarding of the identification numbers when necessary.
4. The system must display on demand a list of all items charged to a borrower.

Charge Circulation Subsystem Requirements

1. The system must quickly identify eligible borrowers and block delinquent or ineligible borrowers through audible and visual alarms.

2. The system must alert the library staff when an item being charged is not on file, is already in circulation, has a hold requirement, or has other exceptional conditions.

3. The library staff must be able to alter the established due dates when necessary.

4. The system must allow the staff to charge out noncirculating items such as reference to borrowers when necessary.

Hardware Maintenance Requirements. Detailed requirements for hardware maintenance can be prepared and included in an RFP. The staff of the library's data processing or computer center or a consultant can be helpful in developing these specifications. The following are some sample requirements for hardware maintenance specifications by various libraries in their RFPs:

1. The vendor must agree to maintain all equipment delivered in good operating condition over the period of the hardware maintenance contract year.

2. All-expense, flat-rate remedial maintenance must be available from 8:00 a.m. to 5:00 p.m., Monday through Friday, excluding dates mutually agreed upon by the vendor and the library.

3. Normal remedial maintenance contact by vendor maintenance personnel must be guaranteed to be within one hour after notification of need, with remedial work to begin within 5 hours after vendor contact, except in circumstances mutually agreed to by the vendor and the library.

Software Maintenance Requirements. Detailed requirements for software maintenance to be acquired can be prepared and included in the RFP. The staff of the library's data processing or computer center or a consultant can again be helpful in developing these specifications. The following are some sample requirements for software maintenance specified by various libraries in their RFPs:

1. The vendor must agree to maintain all application software delivered, including future software enhancements, in good operating condition over the period of the software maintenance contract year.

2. The vendor must upgrade the library's application software as it develops improvements.

3. The vendor must have technical support staff available by telephone during all hours the library is open to the public.

4. The vendor must respond within 2 hours to the problems with the application software and provide corrections or estimates of time for corrections within 8 hours from the time a problem is reported by the library.

Other Vendor Assistance Requirements. The library might wish to obtain other vendor assistance such as installation of a system, training of staff, and provision of training and documentation manuals. Requirements for these services can be included in an RFP. The following are some sample requirements for vendor assistance specified by various libraries in their RFPs:

1. The vendor must provide a training plan to include the necessary formal training of library staff listed in Table Y, for the time periods shown and with the expected competencies listed.

2. The vendor must describe each course or training session for each type of staff, with bid prices for such courses and sufficient information for the library to establish travel and living expenses, if necessary, to attend the courses.

3. Follow-up training must be provided by the vendor, upon mutual agreement by the vendor and the library.

4. The vendor must provide the library with a consolidated set of documents which describe all software and its detailed technical specifications, including all revisions and enhancements for a period of 5 years from the date of installation.

Instructions to Vendors for Submitting Responses. The format for a vendor's response to the library's RFP should be included in the document. The following are typical instructions:

1. *Proposal Summary.* The vendor can be asked to include a brief summary of its response. The summary can serve as an overview or introduction to the document being submitted to the library in response to the RFP.

2. *Vendor Profile.* The vendor can be asked to provide any facts it wishes about the company. The library might require information about the financial stability of the company, the current number of employees, and the names and backgrounds of the staff who will be working with the library. Copies of the firm's latest annual report, independent audit, or Dun and Bradstreet current rating can be requested.

3. *Response to Requirements.* Detailed responses to the lists of requirements of the library for hardware, software, maintenance, and/or other services to be acquired should be included. Each requirement should be responded to by the vendor, with either a "yes" or "no," with brief narrative statements describing the item which would be provided or with references to brochures or technical manuals to be provided.

4. *Special Conditions or Terms.* The vendor can be asked to specify any special conditions or terms that apply to its response.

5. *Environmental and Physical Specifications.* The vendor can be asked to supply details for any space, air conditioning, electrical power, security, environmental impact, or other conditions which will be required to support or house the proposed hardware or software.

6. *Vendor User List.* The library can require that each vendor responding to the RFP submit a list of users of the proposed hardware or software. The list should include the names and addresses of the organization; the name, title, and telephone number of a contact person; the installation configuration and type of work being performed; and the date of the installation. The library may require that only nearby users, or users within a specified geographic area, be listed.

7. *Cost Data.* The vendor can be asked to submit itemized cost data in a specified format. Copies of any forms or formats to be used can be included in the instructions or an appendix to the RFP. In addition, the vendor may be requested to include a general price list of its hardware and software, in case the library wishes to consider or add to the hardware and/or software in the RFP.

8. *Supporting Data.* The vendor can be asked or encouraged to submit other relevant information with a response, such as technical manuals, brochures, photographs, and schematics.

DECISION RULES FOR SELECTING THE BEST RESPONSE

The best response by a manufacturer or vendor should be the one which most closely matches a set of criteria or decision rules established during or immediately after development of the RFP document. These rules, which are similar to those used in chapter 3 to select the best system during system evaluation and comparison, serve as the basis for judging which responses received from vendors are the best. As a standard against which each response will be evaluated, they provide an intelligent basis for selecting one response over another. The following are examples of common criteria or decision rules for selecting the best response:

1. Choose the vendor which meets all or most of the mandatory requirements established for hardware, software, maintenance, and/or other vendor assistance.
2. Choose the vendor which meets all or most of the desirable but not mandatory requirements for the hardware, software, maintenance, and/or other vendor assistance.
3. Choose the vendor which offers the least cost for hardware, software, maintenance, and/or other vendor assistance.
4. Choose the vendor which will be able to meet the library's delivery or installation schedules.
5. Choose the vendor which can best pass a benchmark test (which should be described in detail—see the evaluation techniques described below).

A draft set of decision rules can be prepared and circulated to members of the project advisory committee and others for their comments and suggestions. Ideas and suggestions should be incorporated into a revised draft for formal presentation to the project advisory committee for their discussion, further refinement, and approval.

SOLICITATION OF RESPONSES TO AN RFP

After the project advisory committee and the library's purchasing agency or agencies have developed and approved the request for proposal, they must distribute copies to solicit responses from manufacturers or vendors. There are several methods of identifying potential respondents to whom the RFP can be sent, including:

1. Asking the staff of the data processing or computer center and purchasing department or agency serving the library to suggest names of manufacturers or vendors.
2. Asking colleagues and friends for the names of manufacturers or vendors.
3. Visiting exhibits or booths of vendors and manufacturers at professional conferences and meetings.
4. Examining literature of library and information science, computers, and data processing.

A combination of approaches is necessary to compile the mailing list. Sending a copy of the RFP to every manufacturer or vendor of computer hardware in a list or directory can be expensive and probably will be fruitless, since not all firms sell the appropriate equipment and not all firms respond routinely to such RFPs. The library's data processing or computer center or purchasing agency staff can assist in eliminating those vendors who probably will not respond to or should not be sent the RFP.

Rarely is a request for proposal so complete and clear that potential respondents will not need additional or clarified information. The library should insist that all such inquiries be in writing, for legal and documentation purposes. Vendors may wish to visit the library for briefings or to make presentations or demonstrations of their hardware or software. These requests should be welcomed and honored by the library as a supplement to—not as a substitute for—a formal response to the RFP.

VALIDATION OF RESPONSES FROM VENDORS

Once received from manufacturers or vendors, responses to an RFP must be validated and the best selected. If desired, a consultant can be retained to select or assist in selecting the best response.

The Evaluation Team. A team to evaluate responses from vendors and determine which is best must be selected. The team can consist of, for example, the project manager and the project advisory committee. Assistance from the staff of the data processing or computer center serving the library can be secured, particularly if the RFP responses to be evaluated involve computer hardware. If an outside consultant is to evaluate the responses and recommend the best vendor, then a local evaluation team is of course unnecessary.

<u>Evaluation of Responses from Vendors</u>. The evaluation team must weigh each vendor response to the library's RFP against the set of decision rules established earlier in order to select the best response. The evaluation team should attempt to be as objective as possible in selecting the best response, and may find a combination of methods or techniques necessary.

1. A chart can be prepared for technical comparison of system components. The technical aspects of components to be compared are listed along the left side of the chart, and the names of the vendors to be compared are listed along the top (see Chart K-2 of Appendix K). The responses from each vendor are examined and evaluated carefully, and the data are entered in the chart under the vendor's name and opposite the aspect being considered. The chart can be further examined to determine which vendor's product is best.

2. A chart for technical comparisons can be prepared similar to Chart K-2 to Appendix K, with an additional feature. Each response by a vendor is assigned a score on a scale of 1 to 10 or from 1 to 100, on the basis of a comparison between the library's requirements and the stated characteristics of the vendor's response (see Chart K-2 of Appendix K). For example, if the library requires a minimum internal storage size of 256K bytes, and Vendor A proposes 256K, Vendor B 256K, Vendor C, 192K, and Vendor D, 128K, then the library might rank them with values of 10, 10, 5, and 3 respectively. The scores for all system components are totaled and indicated in the chart. Theoretically, the vendor with the highest numerical score should be the best. (If desired, the lowest rather than the highest numerical ranking can be considered the best response. In this case, the vendor with the lowest numerical score should be the best.) The problem with this type of evaluation is that the numerical rankings might be subjectively made, in which case the comparisons can be suspect.

3. A "yes-no" chart can be prepared for comparing the library's requirements to the responses received from vendors. The mandatory and desirable requirements in the RFP are listed along the left side of the chart and the names of the vendors to be evaluated, along the top (see Chart K-1 of Appendix K). As the responses to the RFP are examined, a "yes" or "Y" is entered in the chart under the vendor's name and opposite the requirement being evaluated if it meets the specification, and "no" or "N" if it does not. Brief explanatory notes can be added in footnotes or within the "yes-no" response as needed.

4. A cost comparison chart can be prepared (see Chart K-3 of Appendix K). The system components or features are listed along the left side of the chart and the names of the vendors to be evaluated, along the top. As the response of each vendor is evaluated, the cost of each component or feature is determined and the cost entered in the chart. The totaled costs for each vendor are indicated at the bottom of the column.

5. If the benchmark technique is used, each vendor is given a job or problem to be solved by its hardware and/or software and the results are recorded and evaluated by the evaluation team. For example, each vendor might be given the job of charging out, renewing, and discharging a number of items to a number of borrowers, under varying conditions and with stated response time limits. This technique can readily weed out those vendors whose systems are not operational and provides an effective means of evaluating functional, time, and processing load requirements of the library. However, the benchmark problem must be carefully selected in advance to represent the true conditions desired by the library, and interpreting the results of the test can be difficult. Since such benchmark problems would require that the tests be run in actual operating conditions, the evaluation team might have to travel to different locations to see the problems solved. Prospective vendors cannot be expected to ship and install equipment and software in the library merely for such a test. Care should be taken to insist that the test job or problem be simulated on the same equipment configuration which would be supplied to the library. This technique obviously requires much advance thought and planning in order to yield good results.

Selection of the Best Response to an RFP. Once all responses to the RFP have been evaluated, the best can be chosen. A chart can be prepared to facilitate and document the decision-making process when the best system is selected. The names of the vendors are listed along the top of the chart, and headings such as "meets all requirements," "comparison of hardware," and "total costs bid" can be placed along the left side (see Chart K-4 of Appendix K). After the results of the evaluation are summarized and transferred onto the chart, the chart can be studied to determine which is the best response to the RFP.

The Evaluation Report. The evaluation team should prepare a report summarizing the validation process and recommending the best response to the library's RFP. This document should include as a minimum:

1. An introduction, in which a brief background or summary of the evaluation is given.
2. The set of decision rules established for selecting the best response to the RFP.
3. A list of the vendors who responded to the RFP.
4. The names and qualifications of the evaluation team.
5. A step-by-step discussion of the evaluation process(es) used and the results, including copies of charts.
6. The recommendation of the best vendor, with a discussion or rationale for the decision if desired.

A sample report of the evaluation of an RFP can be found in Appendix K.

CONTRACT NEGOTIATION

After responses to the RFP have been evaluated and the best hardware, software, or system selected, the library must negotiate a contract with the successful bidder. Many or all of the contractual expectations should have been included in detail in the RFP itself, and a vendor's responses can be considered part of the contract. A contract should include as a minimum:

1. A complete, detailed list of all hardware, software, and/or other vendor assistance to be supplied.
2. The terms and conditions of hardware and software maintenance to be supplied.
3. A complete, detailed calendar or schedule of times for delivery of all contracted items.
4. A complete, detailed description of the method of financing the hardware, software, and other items and a schedule of payments.
5. If desired, penalty clauses for nondelivery or late delivery of contracted items.
6. A clear indication of who owns title to hardware and software, the resale rights of the library, and the rights of the library to modify or change software.
7. An indication of any performance bonds which must be posted by the vendor.
8. A description of the warranties or guarantees on hardware and software and their time lengths.
9. The terms of final acceptance of the hardware and software by the library.

Chapter 7
System Implementation

The purpose of system implementation is to install, activate, evaluate, and accept the new system being developed. This phase is the culmination of a project and is essential regardless of the type, size, or nature of computer-based system being developed.

Specifically, this chapter includes discussions of:

- Space layout.
- Site preparation.
- Job descriptions.
- Staff orientation and training.
- Library patron orientation.
- Acquisition of special supplies, equipment, and forms.
- File creation and conversion.
- Installation and check of hardware and software.
- System activation.
- System evaluation and acceptance.

The plan for project completion prepared earlier should be reviewed at this time and revised to incorporate any actual or anticipated changes. The project schedule should also be reviewed at the same time and revised accordingly to reflect more accurately the timetable for completing the activites during this phase.

SPACE LAYOUT

Good layout of floor space is critical to the efficient, effective operation of a new system to be installed. Charts should be prepared for the physical arrangement of hardware, equipment, and furniture in the in-house computer room and for the remaining space required by the new system, using the exact installation information obtained from the manufacturers or vendors. The exact location of each piece of hardware, equipment, and furniture as well as the relationship of individual work stations to each other must be indicated. Design of space layout can be accomplished as development of site preparation specifications proceeds.

If an in-house computer is to be installed, a space layout chart should be prepared for the space to house it. Some general considerations for space layout include the following:

1. Specifications of the manufacturer or vendor for particular placement and spacing of equipment should be followed.
2. The arrangement should increase efficient use of the space.
3. Sufficient space around equipment should be allowed for easy operation and maintenance.
4. Space should be allowed for an adequate flow of people and materials between work stations.
5. The layout should be as flexible as possible for future expansion or modification.
6. Recognized safety specifications for entrances and exits and access to them should be followed.

The boundaries of the space for the computer room can be drawn on grid paper or on blank paper, using a scale of one-tenth, one-fourth, or other reasonable length to one foot of floor space. The location of all doors, windows, and columns should be precisely indicated. Model cutouts of each piece of hardware, equipment, and furniture can be prepared to the same scale and positioned on the chart until a proper and pleasing arrangement meeting all the many specifications has been achieved. Once the best arrangement has been determined, the cutouts can be glued to the chart. Later modifications to the layout may be necessary as installation specifications are prepared. In fact, space layout and site specifications probably will be prepared simultaneously. Layout for a typical in-house computer room is shown in Figure 7-1.

A layout chart should also be constructed for other space required for the new system being implemented, using the same techniques and considerations as for the in-house computer center. Flexibility and the ease of work flow and communications through the physical space should be emphasized. A layout flowchart, shown in Figure 7-2, can assist in locating traffic patterns and reducing traffic congestion and movement of work through the system. Lines showing anticipated movement of people, information, and materials are superimposed on a space layout chart, with arrowheads pointing the direction of flow of work. If separate flows for different people, information, or materials are necessary, different colors can be used for each. The separate work flows from work station to work station can be identified by numbers keyed to a chart legend.

Figure 7-1. Layout for a typical in-house computer room.

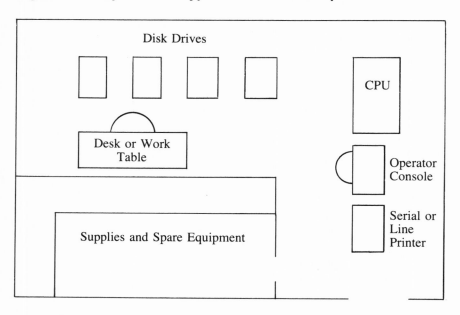

Figure 7-2. A sample layout flowchart depicting the path or flow of work in a room.

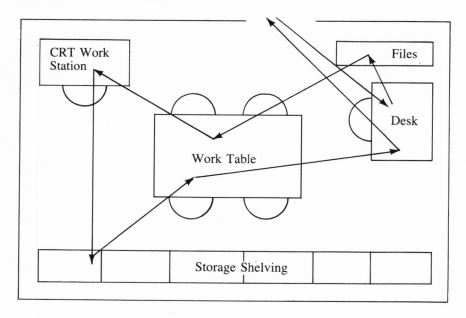

SITE PREPARATION

When the site preparation specifications and the space layouts have been completed and approved, the site preparation itself can be begun. This site preparation can be as simple as rearranging a few pieces of equipment and furniture and installing new electrical outlets or as complex as renovating and refurbishing complete rooms. The extent of the preparation depends upon the nature and complexity of the new system to be implemented. The work includes making ready the physical space for an in-house computer and/or a new system and arranging the hardware, equipment, and furniture so that the new system can be operated effectively and efficiently in the allotted space.

A set of specifications must be developed for those who will prepare the site for a computer-based system. Most if not all these specifications are supplied by the hardware and equipment manufacturers or turnkey system vendors. They should be followed precisely for best results— particularly because in many cases warranties can be voided if the proper installation specifications are not followed carefully. A turnkey system vendor and local engineers, electricians, carpenters, heating and air conditioning specialists, and others can be consulted in preparing the specifications for the site. Of concern are electrical power, temperature, humidity, walls, partitions, ceilings, storage facilities, lighting, safety and security, fire detection, and cabling specifications. A sample set of specifications for preparing a computer room site is shown in Appendix L.

Hardware Installation Specifications. The designer should review system design specifications before beginning to develop site preparation specifications. Thus she or he will be familiar with the space needs in general for the new system and can identify the in-house computer system hardware, if any, and other hardware and equipment to be installed for the new system. A checklist of hardware and other equipment for typical computer-based systems is shown in Appendix I.

The designer must obtain specifications for installation and operation of all hardware required by the new system before developing site preparation specifications. If necessary, the designer can write or telephone the manufacturers or vendors for detailed installation specifications. The information which should be obtained for each piece of hardware and equipment for site preparation planning includes the following, when applicable:

1. Dimensions (width, depth, and height).
2. Space clearance required all sides and top of hardware.

3. Weight.
4. AC power requirements (amps, volts, phases, wattage).
5. Heat generated (BTU/hour maximum).
6. Tolerable operating temperature range.
7. Tolerable operating relative humidity range.
8. Power cord length.
9. Power cable plug description or receptacle required.

This information, some of which may already have been collected during previous phases of the project, should be arranged and organized in a file or notebook for quick, easy reference during preparation of the site specifications.

Selection of a Site for an In-House Computer. If an in-house computer is to be installed, a site must be selected for it. The site selected will depend upon the space arrangements and their priorities within the library, the location of staff who will operate and manage the machines, and geographical dispersion of other branches or libraries, if any, that will share the system. Some general considerations for selecting a site for a computer room within the library include the following. Select a location:

1. In which the computer will be isolated from people who will be bothered by the machines' noise and necessarily lowered temperatures.
2. That is readily accessible to those who will most often have to go to the machines to operate and maintain them.
3. Where adequate temperature, air movement, and humidity can be maintained and controlled.
4. Where adequate security can be maintained (that is, where access by unauthorized persons can be controlled by locked doors or by staff on duty).
5. With no carpeting and away from main sources of dust and dirt such as loading docks.
6. That will be flexible enough to meet future conditions.
7. Whose floor can withstand the weight of the equipment.

Electrical Power Specifications. Electrical power requirements supplied by the manufacturer or vendor should be carefully specified for each piece of hardware and equipment to be installed. The AC power specifications for amps, volts, phases, and wattage, the type of mating receptacle, and the number of receptacles required should be specified for each piece. A library which has problems receiving a continuous, even flow of electrical energy due to fluctuations, surges, and brownouts might need to install a transformer, voltage regulator, or perhaps a standby or emergency power supply or generator in order to provide adequate uninterrupted energy for an in-house computer.

Temperature Specifications. The tolerable temperature range to be maintained and the maximum BTU (British thermal unit) output per hour for each piece of hardware and equipment should be specified. Except for good air flow around equipment, no special temperature specifications are necessary for CRT and typewriter terminals and other peripheral equipment, but with an in-house computer one of the more troublesome problems in a computer-based library system can be temperature control. Ideally, the temperature in a computer room should be held in the 60 to 70 degree Fahrenheit range. Lower temperatures down to freezing do not affect the operation of the system as much as higher temperatures do. Excessive heat can lead to malfunctions of the hardware and can shorten its lifetime or permanently damage the computer. Air flow around pieces of computer hardware also is important, because heat builds up around the equipment and must be dispersed as rapidly and evenly as possible. Since it is recommended that a computer run 24 hours a day, the air conditioning must also run around the clock. If the library's air-conditioning system is not reliable, auxiliary or backup systems may be necessary.

Humidity Specifications. Relative humidity in an in-house computer room should be specified to remain within a range of 40 to 60 percent. Excessive humidity can easily corrode the mechanical parts of most computer hardware, such as CRTs and typewriter terminals. Static electricity tends to build up around disk drives, tape drives, and other moving parts of a computer system when the humidity drops below 40 percent, and either low or high humidity can change the operating characteristics of magnetic disks and tapes, thus potentially causing misreads of stored data. Maintenance of a proper humidity level and antistatic mats can eliminate these problems. Other hardware and equipment such as modems and CRT terminals need no special humidity controls under normal room conditions in an air-conditioned space, although the same 40–60 percent range should be maintained if possible.

Partition and Ceiling Specifications. There are no special requirements for constructing or remodeling walls, partitions, and ceilings for a computer-based library system, except that local building codes should be followed. For an in-house computer room, sound absorption and temperature retention insulation should be used as liberally as possible.

Storage Facilities Specifications. Adequate storage facilities in an in-house computer room must be provided for disk packs not being used, magnetic tapes, paper and forms, printer ribbons, cleaning supplies, spare parts, backup hardware, and other supplies essential to maintaining and operating the computer system. A small room with shelves adjoining the computer room is ideal for this purpose, but shelves along the computer room wall or storage cabinets are also adequate. If magnetic materials are to be stored, the temperature and humidity should be maintained at a level similar to that for the computer itself. Magnetic materials should also be protected from dust and stray magnetic fields. Wooden shelves should be used if possible for storage of such materials.

Lighting Specifications. Normal room lighting is adequate for an in-house computer room, and lighting needs in other areas vary depending upon the tasks to be performed at specific work stations. Since glare on the glass screens of CRT terminals is a problem, some experimentation with lighting levels and positioning of the equipment may be necessary before this problem can be resolved completely. The lighting handbook of the Illumination Engineering Society can be consulted for proper lighting levels for various tasks.

Cabling Specifications. Special cables are necessary in an in-house computer room to supply power to the various pieces of hardware and to interconnect the devices. A particular type of cable is necessary to transmit signals and data from the computer to CRT or typewriter terminals and other devices in different parts of the building or in other remote locations. The manufacturer or vendor will specify the exact cable type to be used. Since cables might have to be strung along or under floors, in ceilings, and up walls, estimates of the cable length requirements should take into consideration the exact paths over which the wires must be laid. Unspliced cables are required in most instances.

Floor Specifications. In most circumstances, the flooring is already adequate for an in-house computer room and for work stations housing computer terminals and other equipment. However, a qualified engineer should check the floor before heavy computer equipment is installed, particularly if the subfloor is not prestressed or reinforced concrete. In some computer centers, raised flooring is installed to redistribute the weight of the hardware and conceal numerous power cords and cables. However, in most libraries which will house only a small computer with limited peripheral equipment, existing flooring should suffice. Power cords and cables can be placed behind equipment where people will not ordinarily be moving, and cable bridges can be installed to protect the wires and maintain a neat appearance in the room.

Vinyl or similar tile floor covering is recommended for an in-house computer room to eliminate or minimize static electricity, but carpeting with a static eletricity level below 2,000 static volts is acceptable. Anti-static mats can be placed on carpeting in front of hardware such as magnetic disk and tape drives which will be most affected by static electricity.

The floor, whether tile or carpeting, must be vacuumed—not swept—regularly to eliminate dirt and dust.

Safety and Fire Specifications. Local safety and fire codes should be followed in preparing the site for an in-house computer room and for other hardware and equipment supporting a computer-based system. Fire and smoke detectors should be installed if possible, and fire extinguishers for Class C (electrical) fires should be provided in a computer room and close to other hardware and equipment. All materials, paints, tiles, carpeting, etc. to be used should be specified as flame or fire retardant.

Security Specifications. Since computer hardware, other specialized equipment, software, and data files are valuable, adequate protection from unauthorized people should be provided. The in-house computer room should remain locked at all times authorized staff are not present, particularly if the public could ordinarily gain entrance to the areas. Other equipment should be placed only where it will be constantly in use by library staff or where its use can be monitored closely for misuse or vandalism. Extreme instances of theft, sabotage, or vandalism cannot be prevented in libraries, but commonsense precautions should be taken to limit the public's access to hardware and equipment which could be damaged or destroyed.

Site Work Initiation. The site preparation must be initiated by the project manager. How this is accomplished depends upon the rules and regulations governing the library's powers and capabilities. Some libraries can initiate such work by simply forwarding work orders along with the required layouts and specifications to the appropriate departments within its parent organization or institution, while others must go through a process of soliciting, receiving, and evaluating bids before awarding a contract for the work. Some libraries can have some of the site preparation completed by local maintenance staff, while other work must be contracted out.

Site Preparation Monitoring and Approval. Once site preparation has been initiated, the work should be monitored to ensure that specifications and timetables are being adhered to. The project manager should inspect the site at regular and frequent intervals and be available at all times to answer questions from those who are performing the work. After the site has been prepared, the work must be accepted or approved before payment is made and before installation of any hardware and equipment can proceed. The work should be checked carefully against the layout charts and the site preparation specifications. Oversights or work improperly performed should be corrected before approval of the site is given.

JOB DESCRIPTIONS

A separate job description—a written record of a staff position and its requirements—is needed for each class, type, or level of staff who will be working in the new system. A job description usually includes:

1. The job title or name.
2. The division, department, and section or unit to which the job is assigned.
3. The person to whom the person filling the position reports.
4. The number and types of staff members, if any, to be supervised.
5. A brief summary statement of the work performed, including the function or purpose and scope of the position.
6. A detailed listing of the specific duties or tasks assigned to the job.
7. The skills and training essential for the job, including the equipment to be operated.
8. The physical demands of the job.
9. A brief and general description of the working conditions.

Other points can be included if thought necessary. The job descriptions will be used in organizing the work to be performed in the new system and in hiring, training, and evaluating the staff. Two sample job descriptions for positions in a computer-based library system are shown in Appendix M.

STAFF ORIENTATION AND TRAINING

Installing any new system in the library is disruptive for both staff and patrons. Introducing a new computer-based system can particularly be traumatic because it involves technology and procedures requiring use of machines which some people fear and distrust. The success of any new system depends to a great extent upon the cooperation and interest of the staff who manage, operate, and use it; therefore, it behooves library management to include a well-planned, well-executed orientation and training program in the system development process.

Development of User Documentation. Adequate user documentation is essential to the proper training and orientation of staff and to their later effective management and operation of the new system after it has been installed.

A general orientation manual or guide can provide the staff and others with an overview of the system, explaining how it operates and why. This type of documentation is the beginning point for staff orientation and training and should include:

1. The purposes and objectives of the new system.
2. A schematic depicting the various subsystems into which the system is broken.
3. Brief narrative descriptions of each subsystem.

This overview manual or guide might be included as an introduction to the detailed procedure manuals described below. A sample of a general orientation guide for a circulation system can be found in Appendix N.

A detailed procedure manual should be prepared to provide the staff with a narrative or overview description of each procedure and step-by-step instructions on how to operate and manage each subsystem of the new system. This type of documentation serves:

- As an instructional tool or training manual for familiarizing new staff with the system.

- As a historical reference of the system for future modifications and improvements to the system.

- To eliminate future distortion of the system by ensuring that procedures are performed in a standard way.

A part of a sample procedure manual for a circulation system is shown in Appendix O.

Hardware and equipment guides should be obtained from the manufacturer or vendor or developed locally to train staff how to operate the devices they are expected to use and to serve as a troubleshooting reference, when necessary, to maintain the machines in good operating condition. The guides should include:

1. A diagram of each device with a legend describing the parts and their purposes or functions.
2. Brief yet clear instructions for operating each device.
3. Instructions for checking the equipment and correcting problems when malfunctions occur.

A sample guide for a piece of hardware is shown in Appendix P.

Planning the Orientation and Training Program. Most of the instruction in the orientation and training program is based upon the previously developed user documentation. However, the program should be planned in advance and well coordinated to achieve maximum results. The following must be decided:

1. Specifically what each individual staff member should know about the new system. If desired, the staff can be divided into groups such as supervisors, terminal operators, computer operators, and so on, and the needs of each category determined appropriately.
2. Whether orientation and training will consist of formal classroom courses, individual tutoring, self-teaching, or a combination of methods.
3. Who will conduct or administer each segment of the orientation and training.
4. If the orientation and training will be at a site outside the library (in a manufacturer or vendor's facilities, for example), in a conference room in the library, at each individual work station, or elsewhere.

A schedule for the staff orientation and training should be prepared and distributed well in advance of the sessions. General orientation can take place at any time during the implementation phase, but training staff to operate the new system should not be scheduled until the hardware and software have been installed and checked out.

General Orientation Sessions. One or more orientation sessions should be conducted to provide an overview and familiarize staff in general with the new system to be installed. The general orientation guide prepared earlier should be distributed in advance of the sessions. The instructor should summarize the purposes or objectives of the new system and explain the various subsystems and how they function together. Adequate time should be allowed for questions and answers. The staff members probably will be particularly concerned at this time about their individual roles in managing and operating the system.

Additional courses can be organized and conducted for the benefit of those with no knowledge of information processing and computers, or such people can take advantage of courses offered by community colleges, universities, professional organizations, or equipment manufacturers and vendors. Individuals can also use programmed texts and courses to better understand automation. Tours of computer centers and other libraries with computer-based systems can be organized.

Training Staff to Operate Equipment. The previously developed equipment operating guides can be used to train those staff who will be operating the computer, printers, CRT or typewriter terminals, and other devices which are part of the new system. This type of training might also be supplied by the vendor or manufacturer of the equipment. Many of them offer such training periodically during the year at strategic locations across the country, usually at nominal or no cost to the library except for transportation, lodging, and meals. Some vendors bring the training to the library, depending upon contractual arrangements made during the hardware and software acquisition. Staff should first be trained until they are confident that they can operate the equipment adequately. Once they are familiar with the devices and their operation, staff then can concentrate on mastering the system that uses the equipment.

Training Staff to Operate the System. Once staff have learned how to operate the necessary equipment, they must be taught to operate the system that uses the equipment. The detailed procedure manuals developed previously should be given to the staff well in advance of the training sessions, in order to give them time to read, study, and formulate questions.

During the training session, the procedures should first be explained in an overview session, with opportunities for questions and answers at that time. Then, each staff member should be given an opportunity for hands-on experience with the equipment, following the step-by-step instructions and using test data or records. The trainer should be available to provide encouragement, correct incorrect actions, and coach the learner in the individual tasks to be performed.

Follow-Up Orientation and Training. Follow-up sessions should be conducted as necessary to repeat the general orientation, reinforce the training, allow identification and correction of problems encountered during the first sessions, and enable the staff to ask additional questions, now that they have more confidence and have the initial traumas of learning something new behind them. The general orientation guide, detailed procedure manuals, and equipment operating guides should be revised, if necessary, to reflect new ideas gained during the initial orientation and training and to correct inadequate descriptions of the new system or its equipment and their operation.

LIBRARY PATRON ORIENTATION

The library's users or patrons are the ultimate benefactors, either directly or indirectly, of a new computer-based system. Invariably, there are conversion and installation problems which might adversely affect services to them on a temporary basis. Inconveniences can be minimized by a good public relations or publicity program initiated well in advance of the new system's installation. Then, when problems do arise, patrons can better understand that the inconveniences are temporary and that the new system, once installed and operating successfully, will provide them with better and faster services. The following are some steps that could be taken as part of a public relations program:

1. Place some posters advertising the impending installation of the computer-based system in strategic places in the library, particularly at locations where the public will be in direct contact with the new system.
2. Write and distribute several publicity releases about the new system to local news and radio and television stations. Include photographs of staff or patrons using the new equipment when possible.
3. Ask local newspaper and radio and television stations to send reporters to interview the library director, project manager, and staff about the new system.
4. Prepare simple brochures, bookmarks, and other handouts describing the new system and distribute them at service desks throughout the library.

The program should be started as early in the implementation phase of a project as possible. Publicity releases and interviews should be repeated as often as possible to retain and refresh users' awareness and interest about the new system.

ACQUISITIONS OF SPECIAL SUPPLIES, EQUIPMENT, AND FORMS

Computer and other hardware essential to the operation of the new system should already have been ordered by the time the implementation phase is begun. Other special supplies, equipment, and forms must be acquired before the system is activated.

The special supplies, equipment, and forms needed for the new system will depend upon the type, nature, and size of the system to be installed and whether an in-house computer will be installed. Hardware and software vendors can be helpful in determining what items should be acquired. A checklist of special supplies, equipment, and forms for use with typical computer-based library systems is shown in Appendix Q. General office supplies such as pencils, pens, paper clips, typewriter ribbons, and the like are not included.

How supplies, equipment, and forms identified for acquisition are ordered and from whom varies from library to library, depending upon the rules and regulations governing the purchasing powers and procedures of each library. Some libraries may order from any vendor they choose, while others must order from specific firms using prenegotiated purchasing contracts. Still others must go through a process of advertising and soliciting bids for all purchases. The library's purchasing department or agency should be able to assist in identifying vendors and prices and placing the necessary orders. A number of nationally recognized firms specialize in handling supplies, equipment, and forms for computer-based systems.

The amount of supplies, forms, and equipment also will depend upon the type, nature, and size of the new system to be installed and the amount of funds available to the library. Sufficient supplies and forms to operate the new system for at least a year should be ordered initially if possible.

FILE CREATION

Creation of some machine-readable files is necessary for most computer-based library systems. This activity can be one of the most expensive and time-consuming tasks of new system implementation and should be begun as soon as possible.

File Identification. The machine-readable files to be created for the new system can be identified by reviewing the design specifications for the new system (chapter 5). Only those files which ordinarily must be created prior to system activation are of concern at this time. For example, some files required in machine-readable form for a circulation system might include borrower registration and bibliographic files; some files for an acquisitions system might include vendor name and address and fund files; and some files for a serials system might include vendor name and address, serials holdings, binding, and check-in files. Other files, such as in-circulation, fines, overdues, and on order files, usually are created as a new system operates. In some cases, a small machine-readable file can be created prior to system activation, and records can be added later as funds, time, and staff permit. For example, a small bibliographic file representing only a fraction of the library's holdings can be created before system activation, with the remainder to be converted as the system operates.

Methods of File Creation. A decision must be made as to how each machine-readable file will be built or created. There are 2 basic approaches to this process: creating the files locally, or contracting for file creation with an outside organization or firm.

A combination of the 2 is possible; that is, some files can be created in-house while others can be created by a commercial firm through contractual arrangements. A simple cost study can be conducted to contrast the various alternatives before one is selected. Costs for conversion of machine-readable files usually are computed on a per record basis.

Files can be created locally, either in-house or in a data processing or computer center serving the library, by manually keying data for records, one by one, into punched cards or punched tape, then transferring the data onto a magnetic tape or magnetic disk file. The information also can be keyed directly onto a magnetic disk file using online CRT or typewriter terminals. The advantages to local file creation are that this method might be less expensive than contracting to have the work performed by others, and the library can maintain complete control locally over the quality, quantity, and speed of the conversion. The disadvantages are that staff, equipment, computer programs, and time must be available to the library to have the necessary work performed.

The creation of essential machine-readable files also can be contracted to others such as a commercial firm, a data processing service bureau, or a library network operations office. In such cases several vendors specializing in serving libraries who have access to large-scale bibliographic data bases search their files, copy records for any matches found onto magnetic tape, and send the tape to the library. The library must supply Library of Congress (LC) card numbers, International Standard Book or Serial Numbers (ISBN/ISSN), or other identifying information such as author and title for the records to be retrieved and copied. The advantages to contracting with others for file creation are that the library need not dedicate staff time to the conversion and need not acquire the equipment and software essential for this work. The disadvantages are that the method can be expensive and, without careful planning and negotiation with the vendor, quality might not be assured.

The Conversion Process. Once the method of creating essential machine-readable files has been determined, a timetable for the process can be established and incorporated into the overall project calendar. The schedule must minimize interference with operations in the existing manual system. Data for records to be converted to a machine-readable form may have to be collected, verified, and/or edited before the conversion can begin. Data can be collected on forms designed earlier in the project (chapter 5). In some cases, records such as catalog or shelf list cards can be used as copy for the conversion process. It might be necessary to verify and edit the data on the collection forms or catalog cards for correctness and completeness before records are converted. In some cases, data might have to be added to or deleted from the records before conversion. If a bibliographic data base is to be searched by a contractor, the library must supply lists of LC card numbers, ISBN/ISSN, or other author and title information on sheets or as specified by the vendor.

After data have been collected, verified, and/or edited, records can be forwarded for punching, keying, or retrieval from bibliographic files. Usually, records are processed in groups or batches. Before file creation is complete, records which have been converted to a machine-readable form should be checked or verified to determine that they are correct, complete, and error-free. Detected errors must be corrected.

INSTALLATION AND CHECK OF HARDWARE AND SOFTWARE

The delivery of hardware and software which will support the new system should be scheduled to coincide with the completion of site preparation. If possible, hardware should not even be delivered until the site is ready, although the timetables of manufacturers and vendors often cannot be controlled or predicted in advance. Hardware should not be installed until the site has been prepared and accepted. Prematurely delivered equipment should be left unopened in its crates until the arrival of those who will install the hardware or until the project manager authorizes installation by others.

The project manager should supervise or at least monitor closely the installation of hardware and other equipment to make certain that nothing is damaged and that items are placed in their predetermined locations. Those who install the hardware should conduct general tests to make certain that it is operating normally and properly. The installers should:

1. Unpack, assemble, and clean the equipment.
2. Identify, report, obtain, and install any missing pieces.
3. Place the equipment in designated locations and make certain that it is stable and level, if this is critical.
4. Connect all essential cables and power cords and install cable bridges if necessary to secure cables in place.
5. Energize the equipment.
6. Ascertain that all motors and heat dispersion fans are operating normally.
7. Test the equipment in an operational mode. For a computer, this includes installation and running of system software.
8. Check that all status lights illuminate properly and under the appropriate conditions.
9. Check that all audible and visual alarms are in good working condition.

After hardware has been installed, checked, and certified to be operating normally, the application software to be used should be tested. The purpose of this step is not to train staff or accept hardware or software, but to make certain that essential software will drive the hardware as expected and will perform the expected tasks. Each function in the new system should be checked using test data, and errors or malfunctions should be reported and corrected before staff training is begun and before the new system is actually activated.

SYSTEM ACTIVATION

Once hardware and software have been installed and tested, staff have been oriented and trained, and essential files have been created, the new system can be activated. There are several approaches to activation of a computer-based system, each with its own particular advantages and disadvantages for a specific project:

1. *Total Approach*. In the total or all-at-once approach to new system activation, the old system is abandoned completely on a given date and time and the new system takes its place. This approach is by far the most demanding, and requires careful planning and coordination. Equipment and software must be thoroughly tested and checked and personnel must be well oriented and trained to operate and manage the new system in advance. This approach probably should not be used when the new system involves widely separated elements in the operation, such as branches.

2. *Pilot Approach*. When the library has several relatively self contained and geographically separate branches, it may be better to implement a new system first in only one of the units, on a pilot project basis. This approach permits the selection of the particular organizational unit in which the staff are most ready to accept the new system, while installation in other units of the library need not begin until everyone is satisfied that the pilot installation is running smoothly. The successful operation of the new system in one branch can strongly motivate hesitant staff in other units. The activation of the system on a small scale can usually be accomplished more quickly than for the total system and also permits the overall installation to progress at a more relaxed pace.

3. *Phased Approach*. In the phased approach to system activation, the system is separated into a number of modules or subsystems that are installed one at a time. Although this approach takes

longer, there is more time to work with the problems which arise in the individual parts. Unfortunately, not every system can be installed in this manner because it may not be possible to separate a system into significant, relatively independent subsystems.

4. *Parallel Approach.* The parallel approach to new system activation requires that the old and the new systems operate side by side for a period of time. The old system is gradually or suddenly phased out as soon as the new system is performing satisfactorily. This approach is best when the consequences of failing to produce satisfactory results with the new system would be disastrous. It is the most conservative and costliest of approaches, because 2 systems must be operated simultaneously to perform the same functions. On the other hand, this approach does permit the staff to solve problems encountered with the new system before abandoning the old.

Sometimes, a combination of system activation approaches may be necessary. The project manager should monitor the events very closely to identify and correct problems as they occur.

SYSTEM EVALUATION AND ACCEPTANCE

Finally, the new system must be evaluated and accepted after it has been activated. Acceptance requirements must be developed by the project manager and approved in advance by both the library and the manufacturer or vendor of the system. Some common requirements used by libraries are that the system can be accepted when:

1. It is operating normally and smoothly with satisfactory results or within a specified range of tolerated errors.
2. All specifications outlined in the RFP and/or agreed to in the acquisition contract have been met.
3. The staff can adequately operate and manage the system.
4. The hardware and software have been operating as required for a specified number of consecutive working days with specified minimum downtime.
5. The response time of the installed equipment is within a specified tolerance range.
6. All goals and objectives for the new system have been met.

The library should not fault the system for failing to perform in a manner for which it never was intended or specified by the library. The manufacturer, vendor, or designer can be held responsible only for those requirements or specifications agreed to in advance during the design or acquisition process of the project. A checklist of detailed requirements or factors can be prepared, to which "yes" or "no" responses can be made as the evaluation is made. For example:

1. Is the system running normally and smoothly? (Y or N) _____
2. Have the hardware and software operated for 90 consecutive working days with downtime less than 1 percent? (Y or N) _____
3. Is response time to an inquiry 10 seconds or less with all terminals in operation? (Y or N) _____
4. Are borrowers with overdue materials or fines blocked when they attempt to check out new items? (Y or N) _____
5. Can the operator override a block and thus check out new materials to borrowers if so desired? (Y or N) _____
6. Does the system enable a manual block to be placed against a borrower when necessary? (Y or N) _____
7. Does the system provide on demand a set of statistics for all items currently in circulation, including items checked out today, items circulated this month, and items circulated this year? (Y or N) _____
8. Does the system sense holds placed against items in the discharge function and alert the operator with both audible and visual signals as to what steps to take? (Y or N) _____

The list, which should be exhaustive, can be prepared according to the requirements established for the RFP during hardware and software acquisition. The new system can be evaluated against the checklist by the project manager, the project advisory committee, or a team of representatives from the library and the vendor or manufacturer. The entire system may be evaluated during one session, or the process can be segmented into several sessions during which only one or a few functions or subsystems are evaluated at a time. The hardware and/or software should not be accepted until all requirements have been met.

APPENDICES

Appendix A

A Sample List of Phases, Activities, and Steps for a Project

I. PROJECT PLANNING AND MANAGEMENT

A. Select and appoint a project manager.
   1. Define the abilities desired of the project manager.
   2. Define the duties and responsibilities of the project manager.
   3. Select the project manager.
   4. Appoint the project manager.

B. Establish a project advisory committee.
   1. Define the duties and responsibilities of the committee.
   2. Select the project advisory committee members.
   3. Appoint the members.

C. Develop a long-range plan for automation.
   1. Prepare a draft plan.
   2. Circulate the draft for suggestions and comments.
   3. Incorporate comments into the final document.
   4. Submit the plan for approval.

D. Define the project to be undertaken.
   1. Identify and document the problem or problems facing the library.
   2. Formulate objectives for the project.
   3. Identify and document project constraints.

E. Prepare a plan for project completion.
   1. Prepare a project outline.
   2. Prepare a project schedule.
   3. Define how project progress will be reported.

F. Obtain project approval.
  1. Prepare a draft project initiation document.
  2. Circulate the draft for suggestions and comments.
  3. Incorporate comments into a final document.
  4. Submit the document for approval.

G. Locate and hire a project consultant, if necessary.
  1. Prepare a request for proposal (RFP).
  2. Solicit responses to the RFP.
  3. Evaluate the proposals received.
  4. Select and hire the best consultant submitting a proposal.

H. Identify other project resource people as necessary.
  1. Identify and contact staff of the data processing or computer center serving the library.
  2. Identify and contact hardware and software vendors.
  3. Identify and contact staff in other automated libraries.
  4. Identify and contact representatives of library networks.

II. NEW SYSTEM REQUIREMENTS

A. Study the existing system.
  1. Identify the goals or purposes of the system.
  2. Identify the subsystems of the system.
  3. Study documents and files of the system.
  4. Chart the work flow of the system.
  5. Determine the amount of work performed in the system.
  6. Identify the resources required by the system.
  7. Chart the system's physical space.
  8. Establish the costs of operating the system.
  9. Organize the results for later use.

B. Establish the goals of the new system.
  1. Draft a set of goals.
  2. Circulate the draft for suggestions and comments.
  3. Submit the goals for approval.

C. Identify requirements for the new system.
  1. Identify general requirements.
  2. Identify functional requirements.
  3. Identify work and performance requirements.

D. Obtain approval of the requirements.
  1. Prepare a draft set of requirements.
  2. Circulate the draft for suggestions and comments.

3. Incorporate the comments into the draft.
4. Submit the set of requirements for approval.

III. SYSTEM EVALUATION AND COMPARISON

A. Establish decision rules for selecting the best system.
   1. Prepare a draft of proposed decision rules.
   2. Obtain approval of the rules.

B. Prepare a list of alternative systems to be considered.
   1. Conceptualize the various methods of developing a new system.
   2. Identify alternatives for the list.
   3. Obtain approval of the list.

C. Eliminate the alternatives not meeting the library's requirements.
   1. Prepare a data collection chart.
   2. Compare each alternative to the set of requirements.
   3. Enter results in the data collection chart.
   4. Analyze the results of the comparison.

D. Estimate developmental costs for the remaining alternatives.
   1. Prepare a data collection chart.
   2. Identify sources of information for developmental costs.
   3. Estimate design costs for each alternative.
   4. Estimate hardware costs for each alternative.
   5. Estimate application software costs for each alternative.
   6. Estimate system software costs for each alternative.
   7. Estimate site preparation costs for each alternative.
   8. Estimate file conversion costs for each alternative.
   9. Estimate staff training and orientation costs for each alternative.
   10. Estimate other capital costs.
   11. Estimate miscellaneous costs.
   12. Summarize the developmental costs for the alternatives.

E. Estimate operating costs for the remaining alternatives.
   1. Determine the lifespan to be used.
   2. Identify sources of information for operating costs.
   3. Prepare a data collection chart.
   4. Estimate salaries and wages for operating each alternative.
   5. Estimate supply costs for operating each alternative.
   6. Estimate hardware lease costs for operating each alternative.
   7. Estimate software lease costs for operating each alternative.
   8. Estimate hardware maintenance costs for each alternative.
   9. Estimate software maintenance costs for each alternative.

     10. Estimate transaction or service fees for each alternative.
     11. Estimate miscellaneous costs for operating each alternative.
     12. Summarize and analyze the operating costs for the alternatives.

F. Select the best system.
     1. Prepare a decision chart to summarize the analysis results for the alternatives being considered.
     2. Enter the evaluation results onto the chart.
     3. Analyze the decision chart and select the best system.

G. Obtain approval to proceed with the project.
     1. Prepare a report of the evaluation and comparison study.
     2. Submit the report for approval.

IV. SYSTEM DESIGN AND PROGRAMMING

A. Divide the system into subsystems.
     1. Identify and define the major subsystems of the system to be designed.
     2. Identify and define the functions within each major subsystem.

B. Prepare input and output specifications.
     1. Identify the inputs and outputs of each functional subsystem.
     2. Define the purpose of each input and output.
     3. Prepare general specifications for each input and output.
     4. Specify the input and output data requirements.
     5. Prepare preliminary layouts for each input and output.
     6. Specify the frequency and number of each input and output.

C. Prepare processing specifications.
     1. Revise specifications for each functional subsystem.
     2. Prepare decision flowcharts for each functional subsystem.
     3. Prepare narrative descriptions to accompany the flowcharts.
     4. Check for proper interfaces between the functional subsystems.

D. Prepare data base specifications.
     1. Summarize the data requirements of the functional subsystems.
     2. Establish general requirements for the data base.
     3. Identify and describe the files required by the functional subsystems.

E. Prepare other specifications.
     1. Prepare control and security specifications.
     2. Prepare audit trail specifications.
     3. Prepare backup and recovery specifications.

F. Obtain approval of the design.
1. Review all design work for completeness and accuracy.
2. Prepare a draft report and circulate for comments and suggestions.
3. Incorporate comments into a final design report.
4. Submit the design report for approval.

G. Assist with the development of computer programs.
1. Assist in planning the computer programs.
2. Serve as a resource person to the coders during preparation of the computer programs.
3. Submit data to test the computer programs.
4. Serve as a resource person in debugging and correcting the computer programs.
5. Serve as a resource person in program documentation.

V. ACQUISITION OF HARDWARE, SOFTWARE, AND VENDOR ASSISTANCE

A. Develop a request for proposal (RFP).
1. Prepare an introduction to the RFP.
2. Prepare general ground rules for the RFP.
3. Develop detailed hardware requirements.
4. Develop detailed system software requirements.
5. Develop detailed application software requirements.
6. Develop detailed hardware maintenance requirements.
7. Develop detailed software maintenance requirements.
8. Develop detailed requirements for other vendor assistance wanted.
9. Prepare instructions to vendors for submitting responses to the RFP.

B. Establish rules for selecting the best response to the RFP.
1. Prepare a draft set of decision rules.
2. Circulate the draft for comments and suggestions.
3. Obtain approval of the decision rules.

C. Solicit responses to the RFP.
1. Identify vendors to whom copies of the RFP will be sent.
2. Mail copies of the RFP to the vendors selected.

D. Respond to inquiries from vendors about the RFP as necessary.

E. Validate responses from vendors.
1. Select an evaluation team.
2. Evaluate responses to the RFP from vendors.
3. Select the best response.
4. Prepare an evaluation report.

F. Negotiate a contract with the vendor selected to supply hardware, software, or vendor assistance.

VI. SYSTEM IMPLEMENTATION

A. Review and, if necessary, revise the plan for project completion.

B. Develop site preparation specifications.
   1. Obtain hardware installation specifications.
   2. Select a site for the in-house computer, if one is to be installed.
   3. Prepare space layout charts for the in-house computer room.
   4. Prepare space layout charts for other space required by the new system.
   5. Prepare electrical power specifications.
   6. Prepare temperature specifications.
   7. Prepare humidity specifications.
   8. Prepare wall, partition, and ceiling specifications.
   9. Prepare floor specifications.
   10. Prepare storage facility specifications.
   11. Prepare lighting specifications.
   12. Prepare cabling specifications.
   13. Prepare safety and fire specifications.
   14. Prepare security specifications.

C. Prepare the site.
   1. Initiate the site work.
   2. Monitor site preparation.
   3. Approve the site.

D. Prepare job descriptions.
   1. Prepare draft job descriptions.
   2. Circulate the drafts for comments and suggestions.
   3. Incorporate comments into final job descriptions.
   4. Submit the job descriptions for approval.

E. Orient and train the staff.
   1. Develop user documentation.
   2. Plan the orientation and training program.
   3. Conduct general orientation sessions.
   4. Train staff to operate the equipment.
   5. Train staff to operate the system.
   6. Conduct follow-up orientation and training.

F. Orient library patrons.
  1. Plan a public relations program to orient patrons to the new system.
  2. Implement the public relations program.

G. Acquire special supplies, equipment, and forms.
  1. Identify the supplies, equipment, and forms needed for the new system.
  2. Order the supplies, equipment, and forms.

H. Create essential machine-readable files.
  1. Identify the files to be created.
  2. Determine how the files will be created.
  3. Establish a conversion schedule.
  4. Prepare records for conversion, if necessary.
  5. Convert the records.
  6. Check the accuracy of the conversion.

I. Install and check out the hardware and software.
  1. Supervise and/or monitor the installation.
  2. Check out the hardware.
  3. Check out the software.

J. Activate the new system.
  1. Plan the activation process.
  2. Begin operating the new system.

K. Evaluate and accept the new system.
  1. Evaluate the new system.
  2. Accept the new system.

Appendix B
Sample Network Charts for Activities in Appendix A

1. PROJECT PLANNING AND MANAGEMENT

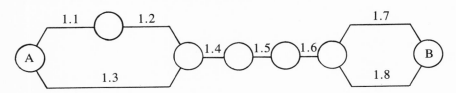

1.1 Select and appoint a project manager.
1.2 Establish a project advisory committee.
1.3 Develop a long-range plan for automation.
1.4 Define the project to be undertaken.
1.5 Prepare a plan for project completion.
1.6 Obtain project approval.
1.7 Locate and hire a project consultant, if necessary.
1.8 Identify other project resource people as necessary.

2. NEW SYSTEM REQUIREMENTS

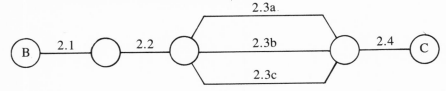

2.1 Study the existing system.
2.2 Establish the goals of the new system.
2.3 Identify requirements for the new system
    2.3a Identify general requirements.
    2.3b Identify functional requirements.
    2.3c Identify work and performance requirements.
2.4 Obtain approval of the requirements.

3. SYSTEM EVALUATION AND COMPARISON

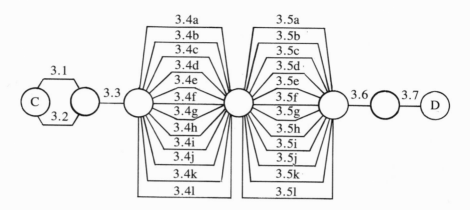

3.1 Establish decision rules for selecting the best system.
3.2 Prepare a list of alternative systems to be considered.
3.3 Eliminate the alternatives not meeting the library's requirements.
3.4 Estimate developmental costs for the remaining alternatives
    3.4a Prepare a data collection chart.
    3.4b Identify sources of information for developmental costs.
    3.4c Estimate design costs for each alternative.
    3.4d Estimate hardware costs for each alternative.
    3.4e Estimate application software costs for each alternative.
    3.4f Estimate system software costs for each alternative.
    3.4g Estimate site preparation costs for each alternative.
    3.4h Estimate file conversion costs for each alternative.
    3.4i Estimate staff training and orientation costs for each alternative.
    3.4j Estimate other capital costs.
    3.4k Estimate miscellaneous costs.
    3.4l Summarize the developmental costs for the alternatives.
3.5 Estimate operating costs for the remaining alternatives
    3.5a Determine the lifespan to be used.
    3.5b Identify sources of information for operating costs.
    3.5c Prepare a data collection chart.
    3.5d Estimate salaries and wages for operating each alternative.
    3.5e Estimate supply costs for operating each alternative.
    3.5f Estimate hardware lease costs for operating each alternative.
    3.5g Estimate software lease costs for operating each alternative.
    3.5h Estimate hardware maintenance costs for each alternative.
    3.5i Estimate software maintenance costs for each alternative.
    3.5j Estimate transaction or service fees for each alternative.
    3.5k Estimate miscellaneous costs for operating each alternative.
    3.5l Summarize and analyze the operating costs for the alternatives.
3.6 Select the best system.
3.7 Obtain approval to proceed with the project.

4. SYSTEM DESIGN AND PROGRAMMING

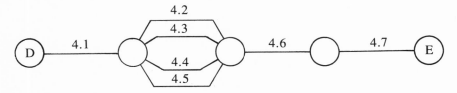

4.1 Divide the system into subsystems.
4.2 Prepare input and output specifications.
4.3 Prepare processing specifications.
4.4 Prepare data base specifications.
4.5 Prepare other specifications.
4.6 Obtain approval of the design.
4.7 Assist with the development of the computer programs.

5. ACQUISITION OF HARDWARE, SOFTWARE, AND VENDOR ASSISTANCE

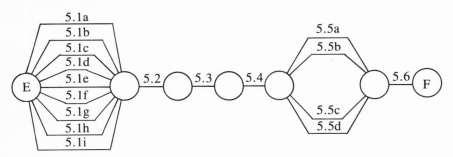

5.1 Develop a request for proposal (RFP)
    5.1a Prepare an introduction to the RFP.
    5.1b Prepare general ground rules for the RFP.
    5.1c Develop detailed hardware requirements.
    5.1d Develop detailed system software requirements.
    5.1e Develop detailed application software requirements.
    5.1f Develop detailed hardware maintenance requirements.
    5.1g Develop detailed software maintenance requirements.
    5.1h Develop detailed requirements for other vendor assistance wanted.
    5.1i Prepare instructions to vendors for submitting responses to the RFP.
5.2 Establish rules for selecting the best response to the RFP.
5.3 Solicit responses to the RFP.
5.4 Respond to inquiries from vendors about the RFP as necessary.
5.5 Validate responses from vendors
    5.5a Select an evaluation team.
    5.5b Evaluate responses to the RFP from vendors.
    5.5c Select the best response.
    5.5d Prepare an evaluation report.
5.6 Negotiate a contract with the vendor selected to supply hardware, software, or vendor assistance.

6. SYSTEM IMPLEMENTATION

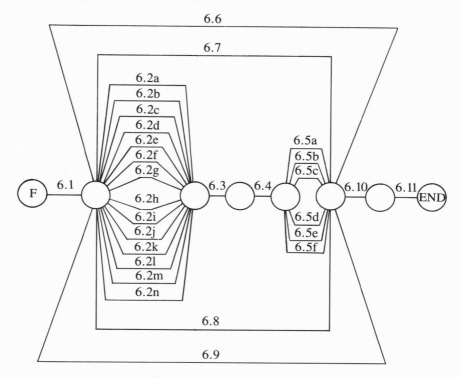

6.1 Review and, if necessary, revise the plan for project completion.
6.2 Develop site preparation specifications
    6.2a Obtain hardware installation specifications.
    6.2b Select a site for the in-house computer, if one is to be installed.
    6.2c Prepare space layout charts for the in-house computer room.
    6.2d Prepare space layout charts for other space required by the new system.
    6.2e Prepare electrical power specifications.
    6.2f Prepare temperature specifications.
    6.2g Prepare humidity specifications.
    6.2h Prepare wall, partition, and ceiling specifications.
    6.2i Prepare floor specifications.
    6.2j Prepare storage facility specifications.
    6.2k Prepare lighting specifications.
    6.2l Prepare cabling specifications.
    6.2m Prepare safety and fire specifications.
    6.2n Prepare security specifications.
6.3 Prepare the site.
6.4 Prepare job descriptions.
6.5 Orient and train the staff
    6.5a Develop user documentation.
    6.5b Plan the orientation and training program.
    6.5c Conduct general orientation sessions.

6.5d Train staff to operate the equipment.
6.5e Train staff to operate the system.
6.5f Conduct follow-up orientation and training.
6.6 Orient library patrons.
6.7 Acquire special supplies, equipment, and forms.
6.8 Create essential machine-readable files.
6.9 Install and check out the hardware and software.
6.10 Activate the new system.
6.11 Evaluate and accept the new system.

Appendix C
A Sample Long-Range Plan for an Automation Program

MISSION OF THE LIBRARY

The mission of the Mount Olympus Memorial Library is to provide its users with access to recorded information. The library has acquired and organized for use a collection of well-selected materials which serves the basic needs of most users, supplemented by agreements and contracts with other libraries and organizations which provide additional information and materials through interlibrary loans. The library also owns sufficient bibliographies and catalogs to enable users to identify and locate virtually any published materials desired. Librarians and other staff are available to assist users in locating, selecting, and obtaining desirable information.

PURPOSES OF AUTOMATION

The goal, objective, or purpose of the library's long-range automation program is to support and assist the library staff in fulfilling its stated mission of providing users with access to recorded information. Specifically, automation will enable the staff to perform as accurately, thoroughly, rapidly, and inexpensively as possible its work of selecting, acquiring, organizing and processing, storing and preserving, locating and retrieving, and disseminating or lending information to the library clientele.

CONSTRAINTS ON AUTOMATION

The computer is to be a tool of the library staff and, ultimately and indirectly, of the user. At no time are humans knowingly to be subjugated to the machine. Rather than humans having to bend to the ways of the computer, the computer must bend to the ways of humans; the machine is flexible enough to do this, given the perseverance of humans.

The total systems approach will be followed in automating the library. That is, all functions or systems within the library are considered to be interdependent and interacting and mutually supportive of the overall mission of the library. Each function or system must interface with all others and provide for the smooth flow of information and work from one to another, on the assumption that output from one will be input to another. Common files or data bases will be used by all functions or systems when possible. Information captured once in a machine-readable form must be used and reused again and again without need for humans to recapture, rekey, or re-record data.

FUNCTIONS TO BE AUTOMATED

Every function or task which can be handled by machines should eventually be automated; this process will take many years, even decades, and might never be fully achieved. The following functions will be automated first, in the priority given and for the reasons indicated:

1. Cataloging. Automation of this function has already been achieved by OCLC, Inc. and others through their shared cataloging systems. Automated cataloging can thus be integrated into Olympus Memorial Library with minimum investment of time and capital by using services of one of these networks. At the same time, maximum benefits will be possible from use of the resulting machine-readable records in other systems.
2. Circulation. There are immediate problems and pressures which automation could alleviate in this highly visible area of the library. This system will be built upon the data base accumulated through the automated cataloging.
3. Interlibrary Loans. An excellent and relatively inexpensive automated interlibrary loan system is now available from OCLC, Inc. The library can build on its participation in this national union catalog of holdings of member institutions. Automation of interlibrary loan can proceed simultaneously with circulation.
4. Acquisitions. The acquisitions system is the point at which materials are identified for incorporation into the library's collections. While logically it might appear that acquisitions should be automated first, the state of the art library automation precludes its early integration into the total program.
5. Online Catalogs. An online catalog will be a by-product of the automated cataloging, acquisitions, and circulation systems. Automation of the catalogs should not be begun until the other systems are implemented and functioning satisfactorily.

These priorities will be reviewed periodically, particularly before each project to develop a new computer-based system is begun.

Appendix D
A Sample Project Initiation Document

PURPOSES AND OBJECTIVES OF THE PROJECT

The primary purpose of this project is to upgrade and improve the effectiveness and efficiency of the library's existing circulation system. Specifically, the objectives of the project are to:

1. Improve services to the citizens using the library by providing faster checkout of materials and thus minimizing queueing at the charge desk.
2. Eliminate all manual filing in the system.
3. Provide a full range of overdue and other notices and reports that will improve services manifold to citizens.
4. Provide better control over materials in circulation.

PROBLEM STATEMENT

The library has had a sharp increase in use of its materials and services in the past few years, and the trend is expected to continue as the population of the community also increases proportionately. While the library has had an increasing number of loans to borrowers, there has not been a corresponding increase in its circulation staff:

	Persons Using Library	Number of Loans	Circulation Staff
1975	40,000	110,980	4.0
1976	65,500	156,777	4.0
1977	91,900	209,080	4.5
1978	111,500	224,523	4.5
1979	124,800	260,129	4.5

As a result, the circulation staff must spend most of their working time charging and discharging materials. Long service queues form at the charging desk; there are long delays in discharging materials after their return; all except first overdue notices have been eliminated because there is no time to prepare them; there are backlogs of records to be merged into the circulation file each day; and the morale of the staff is low because they know they are unable to provide good service.

CONSTRAINTS ON THE PROJECT

This project is the second to be undertaken as a part of the library's long-range plan for automation begun in 1975 and is subject to the general constraints outlined in that document. The following additional constraints or limitations are placed on this particular endeavor:

1. The project manager must prepare and submit a report to the library director after each phase of the undertaking has been completed, and approval by the director must be given before the project is continued further into the next phase.
2. The use of a computer in the new circulation system must be thoroughly justified as being economical and cost-beneficial to the library.
3. The project is expected to be substantially completed by January 19__.

PROJECT MANAGER AND ADVISORY COMMITTEE

David McZeus, Assistant Director for Planning and Systems, will be the manager of the project, and the following staff have been selected to serve on the Project Advisory Committee:

1. Richard Apollo, Associate Director for Public Services.
2. Pallas Athena, Head, Circulation Department.
3. Rosemary Dionysus, Librarian II, Circulation Department.
4. Herschel Theseus, Assistant Director for Bibliographic Control.

The project manager will study the existing system, but a consultant will be selected and hired to complete the remainder of the project.

PLAN FOR THE PROJECT

The following plan is submitted for completing the project; a more detailed plan will be submitted upon approval to proceed. The dates indicated are subject to completion of previous steps and upon approval of the library director and library board.

Obtain approval to initiate the project .... December 15, 19__.
Prepare and mail RFP for securing a project consultant .. December 15, 19__.
Begin study of the existing system .... January 1, 19__.
Proposals from prospective consultants due .... January 1, 19__.
Begin interviewing prospective consultants .... January 15, 19__.
Award contract to the consultant selected .... January 20, 19__.
Consultant to begin work .... February 15, 19__.
Establish requirements for the new system................ March 15, 19__.
Study alternatives and select the system to be developed ...... April 1, 19__.
Prepare RFP for hardware, software, and vendor support ..... May 15, 19__.
Submit RFP for hardware, software, and vendor support ...... June 1, 19__.
Award contracts for hardware, software, and vendor support... July 15, 19__.
Begin implementation of new system.................... October 1, 19__.

PROGRESS REPORTS

Monthly progress reports will be prepared and submitted to the library director and library board. The following reports will be submitted to the director and board for approval as work on the project progresses:

1. The reports of the study of the existing system.
2. A report containing the set of requirements for a new system, a study and comparison of alternative circulation systems which could meet the requirements, and a recommendation of the best and most economical system to be developed.
3. A request for proposal (RFP) for hardware, software, and vendor support.
4. An evaluation report of the bids received in response to the RFP and a recommendation as to which to accept.
5. An implementation report outlining staffing requirements, staff orientation and training, and the special supplies and equipment which must be purchased.

In addition, the project manager will keep the library director and board apprised of any unusual problems and circumstances as they arise.

Appendix E
A Sample Request for Proposal (RFP) for Securing A Project Consultant

INTRODUCTION

Mount Olympus Memorial Library, located on beautiful Mount Olympus, provides library services to its 500,000 users from a central research library of 800,000 volumes, 5 suburban branches, and 10 bookmobiles for outlying areas. The library has a highly qualified staff of librarians, information specialists, and others to provide a full range of services supporting the research and recreational needs of its users.

The library began studying automation of its services 5 years ago and has developed a long-range plan for all projects to develop computer-based systems. The purpose of this particular endeavor is to select, develop, and install an automated circulation system for the library.

STATEMENT OF WORK

The consultant will perform the following tasks for the library:

1. Develop a set of requirements for an automated circulation system to meet the library's needs.

2. Study and compare the alternative circulation systems available, including one developed locally from scratch, and recommend the one which will best meet the requirements of the library and be most cost-beneficial.

3. Prepare a request for proposal (RFP) to acquire the hardware, software, and other services of vendors or manufacturers essential for the circulation system that is recommended.

4. Evaluate the quotations or bids received from vendors or manufacturers for hardware, software, and other services and recommend the offer which the library should accept.

5. Develop an implementation plan for the circulation system recommended, including:
   a. Staffing requirements for the new system.
   b. A staff orientation and training manual.
   c. A set of specifications for the site for the new system.
   d. A checklist of special supplies and equipment which must be purchased for the new system.

REPORTS REQUIRED

The consultant will prepare and submit to the library 10 copies each of the following reports:

1. A report including the set of requirements for the new circulation system (Task A), a summary of the study and comparison of alternative circulation systems, and the recommendation of the best and most economical system to be developed (Task B).

2. The request for proposal (RFP) document for acquiring hardware, software, and other services from vendors and manufacturers (Task C).

3. A report of the evaluation of the quotations or bids received in response to the RFP and the recommendation of the consultant as to which to accept (Task D).

4. Either a single or separate reports on staffing requirements for the new system (Task E1), staff orientation and training (Task E2), and supplies and equipment to be purchased (Task E3).

The consultant will also make verbal monthly reports to the library's project manager describing the work accomplished to date and any unusual problems encountered. In addition, the consultant will apprise the project manager of any unusual circumstances, as they occur, which might delay the work and cause problems later.

PROPOSAL FORMAT

The prospective consultant's response to this RFP should contain the following parts:

1. The consultant's proposed approach or methodology to be followed in completing each of the required tasks in the statement of work above, and the number of working days required to complete each task.
2. The names and qualifications or resumes of all persons, including the prime consultant and including any subcontractors, who will be involved in performing the work outlined in this RFP.
3. A list of names and addresses of libraries for which previous studies have been performed must be included.
4. A detailed summary of the budget proposed for performing the work outlined in this RFP, with each task in the statement of work costed separately in case the library should not have sufficient funds to complete the entire project.

SELECTION OF THE CONSULTANT

Each response to this RFP will be evaluated by a project advisory committee which will select those consultants to be interviewed. Upon completion of the interviews, the committee will select the consultant to undertake the work. The committee will select the consultant using a combination of the following criteria:

1. The best proposed methodology for completing the work within the expected timeframe.
2. The best qualifications for completing the work.
3. The proposal which will result in the least cost to the library.

CONTRACT CALENDAR

The library anticipates a 9-month contract period, beginning January 1, 19__. The following calendar is expected:

Proposals from prospective consultants due by 4:30 p.m..... January 1, 19__.
Begin interviewing prospective consultants............... January 15, 19__.
Award contract to the consultant selected................ January 20, 19__.
Consultant will begin work. .... February 15, 19__.

Report including recommendation of consultant for
circulation system to be developed due in the library. . . . . April 1, 19__.
RFP document for acquiring hardware, software,
and other vendor services due in the library. . . . . May 15, 19__.
The library will issue the RFP to prospective vendors. . . . . June 1, 19__.
Bid documents due in the library by 4:30 p.m. . . . . July 1, 19__.
Report of the evaluation of the bid documents by the
consultant due in the library. . . . . July 15, 19__.
Contract(s) awarded for hardware, software, and
other vendor services. . . . . August 1, 19__.
Final implementation report of the consultant due
in the library. . . . . September 30, 19__.

CONTACT PERSON

David McZeus is the prime contact person for prospective consultants, and all inquiries regarding this RFP and the resulting contract should
be directed to him at the Mount Olympus Memorial Library, 123 Titan
Way, Mount Olympus 12345. Telephone (123) 456-7890.

Appendix F
A Sample Set of Requirements for a Computer-Based Circulation System

The objective of this project is to develop a computer-based circulation system for the library meeting the following specifications or requirements or having the following features.

GENERAL REQUIREMENTS

1. The system must be able to accommodate initially:
   a. Up to 15 branches.
   b. A collection size of 200,000 unique titles.
   c. Up to 15,000 borrowers.
   d. Up to 250,000 circulation transactions per year.
   e. Up to 10,000 holds placed each year.
   f. A minimum of 40 terminals.
2. The system must be able to accommodate double the amounts above without major system redesign or hardware replacement.
3. The system must be able to accommodate software enhancements and expansion of hardware without noticeable disruption to services.
4. The library must be able to add a dial-up facility to the system at a later date without additional internal storage or additional CPU hardware.
5. The system must provide for both input and output of bibliographic data in MARC II format.
6. The privacy of all individuals using the system must be protected at all times.
7. A system of passwords must be provided to control or limit access to all files and functions.
8. The system must be compatible with other automated and manual systems within the library and be as compatible as possible with other local, regional, state, and national systems outside the library.

BORROWER CONTROL

1. The system must provide for entry of data collected about borrowers during their registration.
2. The borrower file must contain for each person registered:
   a. Borrower identification number.
   b. Borrower name.
   c. Street address.
   d. City.
   e. State.
   f. ZIP code.
   g. Telephone number.
   h. Branch where registered.
   i. Date of registration.
   j. Date of last circulation.
   k. Number of items charged.
3. The system must print borrower cards upon demand.
4. The system must delete, upon command, those records for borrowers who do not renew their registrations by specified dates.
5. The system must accept changes, additions, and deletions to any data in records in the borrower file from the terminals.
6. The system must accommodate up to 15 library-designated user types.

CHARGES

1. The system must provide for rapid and accurate charging of materials to borrowers, with response times of 3 seconds average per charge.
2. The system must allow borrower cards to be scanned optically as a means of entering their identification numbers.
3. The system must permit borrower identification numbers to be entered manually on a keyboard as an alternate method of entering the numbers.
4. The system must check borrowers' eligibility to use the library, their borrowing privileges, and their status and alert the operator with both audible and visual prompts of blocks or other unusual circumstances.
5. The system must permit the overriding of blocks when necessary.
6. The system must check the loan period codes for items to be circulated and compute the dates due.
7. The system must permit the overriding of the standard loan periods and setting of different loan periods when necessary.
8. The system must print date-due slips for borrowers.
9. The system must charge out additional items to the same borrower without the operator having to rescan the identification card.

10. The system must allow checkout when necessary of items such as reference materials usually not allowed to circulate.
11. The system must allow checkout of materials to library departments, offices, or other library-designated units.
12. The system must disregard holidays, which shall be specified in advance by the library periodically, in computing dates due.

DISCHARGES

1. The system must provide for rapid and accurate discharging of materials returned by borrowers, with response times of 3 seconds average or less per discharge.
2. The system must sense and trap during the discharge process those items which are overdue or with holds or recalls placed against them.
3. The system must compute and record fines owed if items are overdue and notify the operator with both audible and visual prompts when such situations occur.
4. The system must use the library-specified assessment rates for the different types of borrowers when computing fines.
5. The system must accept and record fines paid on the spot.
6. The system must accept partial payment of fines owed.
7. The system must automatically increase the counter in bibliographic records for the number of times items have circulated.
8. The system must erase borrower identification numbers from the bibliographic and/or circulation files when items have been discharged.
9. The system must alert the operator with both audible and visual signals when items being discharged must be returned to locations outside the library and indicate the branch designations.

RENEWALS

1. The system must complete renewals with or without borrowers' cards and with or without the physical items in hand.
2. The system must check for reserves or holds on items and notify the operator if any exist.
3. The system must follow all other routines or requirements for charges when renewing loans of materials.

HOLDS OR PERSONAL RESERVES

1. The system must accept holds or personal reserves on items in circulation.

2. The system must retain holds on items in the order in which they are placed by borrowers.
3. The system must allow holds to be changed or canceled upon request of borrowers.
4. The system must allow hold queues to be overriden by the staff when necessary.
5. The system must have the ability to place holds on individual copies or all copies of a title.

THE BIBLIOGRAPHIC FILE

1. The system must have the ability to add, change, or delete bibliographic and item records.
2. The system must accept either full or partial records in MARC II format.
3. The item record must contain:
   a. Item/copy identification number.
   b. Item/copy location.
   c. Item/copy cost.
   d. Times the item/copy has circulated.
4. The system must interface with OCLC without additional hardware.
5. The system must provide authority files for main entries and subject headings.
6. The system must have the ability to update the bibliographic file automatically when new or updated main entries or subject headings are added to the authority files.

INQUIRIES

1. The system must allow the rapid determination of titles in the bibliographic file and their locations.
2. The system must allow the rapid determination of titles in circulation and their due dates.
3. The system must allow the rapid determination of holds on items.
4. The system must have a response time of 6 seconds or less for author, title, or patron inquiries, and 10 seconds or less for subject, call number, Library of Congress card number, and ISSN/ISBN.
5. The system must enable searches by author, title, subject, call number, Library of Congress card number, ISBN/ISSN, and patron.
6. The system must allow searches by patron by either patron name or identification number.

7. The system must display items on loan to borrowers during the borrower search.
8. The system must display a "no posting" message if no matches are located during a file search.
9. The system must display a brief listing of all matches to a search argument if more than one match is found, thus enabling the operator to choose the correct one.

NOTICES AND REPORTS

1. The system must prepare and print first, second, and third overdue notices upon demand.
2. The system must prepare and print fine notices upon demand.
3. The system must prepare and print availability notices when necessary.
4. The system must prepare and print a report of all items having exceeded a library-designated number of holds.
5. The system must prepare and print lists of borrowers by either name or ZIP code upon demand.
6. The system must prepare and print a list of materials on loan by units to other units upon demand.
7. The system must prepare and print lists of fines outstanding over library-specified number of days upon demand.
8. The system must prepare and print lists of lost and missing materials upon demand.
9. The system must prepare and print or display upon demand statistics for circulation activity by hours of the day:
   a. By borrower type.
   b. By branch or location.

Appendix G
A Sample Report of a System Evaluation and Comparison

PURPOSE OF THE STUDY

The purpose of this study is to examine and compare the alternative automated circulation systems available to determine which would be the best for development by the library.

METHODOLOGY

Comparing complex computer-based library systems before they are purchased, and sometimes before they are even designed, is hazardous and frustrating due to lack of comparable information and the imprecision of costs before quotations or bids are requested officially. The following methodology, which at least forced a consistency in gathering information, was used in conducting this study:

1. The existing circulation system was studied to determine needs for a new system.
2. A set of preliminary requirements for the new system was developed.
3. Decision rules for selecting the best system from among the alternatives were established.
4. A list of the alternative circulation systems was developed.
5. All alternative systems were compared to the preliminary list of requirements established for the new system.
6. Developmental costs were estimated for the remaining alternatives.
7. Annual operating costs were estimated for the remaining alternatives.
8. The best system was selected, using the decision rules established in step 3 above.

THE EXISTING SYSTEM

The basic function of a circulation system is to provide operational control and related services for the loan of materials to legitimate users of the library. The system must provide continuous control of the more than 800,000 books, microforms, audiovisuals, and other materials in its central research library, 5 suburban branches, and 10 bookmobiles. More than a half-million checkout, check-in, overdue, recall, and fines transactions for over 260,000 loans a year are required by the system. To achieve these ends, the system must:

1. Identify and clear borrowers prior to loan transactions.
2. Check out, check in, and record loans of materials to borrowers.
3. Maintain a data base containing identification, location, and dynamic status information for materials in the library's collections.
4. Locate materials in circulation.
5. Provide for renewal of loans to borrowers.
6. Generate reminders of overdue materials and fines.
7. Record fines owed and fines paid by borrowers.
8. Print lists of delinquent borrowers.
9. Handle holds or personal reserves for items on loan but needed by other borrowers.
10. Collect and compile statistics of various circulation activities.

DECISION RULES

Decision rules were established for selecting the best system to be developed for the library. The best system would be judged to be the one which would:

1. Meet all, or most, of the library's requirements for a new circulation system.
2. Cost the least to develop initially.
3. Cost the least to operate on an annual basis after it is installed.

ALTERNATIVE SYSTEMS STUDIED

Until recently, virtually all computer-based circulation systems were punch-card based, either offline or online, using a large computer outside the library. The advent of bar code labels which can be scanned optically and of small, relatively inexpensive, reliable minicomputers has revolutionized the automation of libraries in just a few short years. The costs of in-house minicomputers in libraries now are highly competitive with manual systems and with those using organizationally separate computer systems.

The following alternatives were identified for examination and comparison in this study:

1. The existing system, because one option available is to retain it and not automate the circulation function at all.
2. The Handy Dandy System, which is a commercial turnkey or off-the-shelf system available from HD Systems, Inc. This system uses a minicomputer which would be programmed at the factory and installed in the library. No programming and other development time is thus necessary on the part of the library, and the vendor provides expert technical support and staff training for the system.
3. The Ultimate Circulation System, which is another commercial turnkey system offered by the UCS Corporation.
4. The Solve-All Circulation System, also a turnkey system available from Solve-It Now, Inc.
5. A system to be designed and developed locally from scratch, which would use the services of the Most-Advanced Data Processing Service Center's computer.

A summary of the comparisons of the alternative systems, excluding the existing system, to the set of requirements established for a new circulation system is shown in Chart G-1. Estimated developmental costs for the alternatives are summarized in Chart G-2, and estimated operating costs for each for a 5-year period, in Chart G-3. The decision chart on which the selection of the best system was based in shown in Chart G-4.

RECOMMENDATION OF THE BEST SYSTEM

The comparison of the 5 alternative systems suggests that the Ultimate Circulation System would be the best system to be developed for the library. This system meets all the library's requirements, as would a system to be developed locally from scratch. The Ultimate Circulation System would cost only $144,730 to develop, while the system developed locally would cost $283,100. While the Handy Dandy System would cost slightly less ($758 less) to operate annually than the Ultimate Circulation System, the Handy Dandy System does not meet several important requirements established by the library, and the combined developmental and cumulative annual operating expenses for 5 years for this system would be $11,767 more than for the Ultimate Circulation System.

Chart G-1. Comparison of Alternative Systems to the Library's Requirements

Requirement*	Handy Dandy System	Ultimate Circulation System	Solve-All Circulation System	System Designed Locally
1. Accommodates 15 branches	Yes	Yes	Yes	Yes
2. Accommodates 200,000 titles	No	Yes	Yes	Yes
3. Accommodates 15,000 borrowers	Yes	Yes	Yes	Yes
4. Accommodates 250,000 annual circulations	Yes	Yes	Yes	Yes
5. Accommodates 10,000 annual holds	Yes	Yes	Yes	Yes
6. Accommodates 40 terminals	No	Yes	No	Yes
7. Can double the amounts above without redesign or hardware replacement	No	Yes	Yes	Yes
8. Acommodates software enhancements and hardware expansions without disruptions	Yes	Yes	Yes	Yes
9. Can add dial-up facility	Yes	Yes	No	Yes
10. MARC II input and output	No	Yes	No	Yes
11. Privacy of individuals retained	Yes	Yes	Yes	Yes
12. Has system of passwords for security	Yes	Yes	Yes	Yes

*Not all requirements shown—sample.

Chart G-2. Summary of Estimated Developmental Costs for the Alternative Circulation Systems

Cost Element	Handy Dandy System	Ultimate Circulation System	Solve-All Circulation System	System Designed Locally
Central processing unit	$39,200	$16,650	$209,000	$35,000
Operator's console	2,500	2,480	*	3,000
Serial printer	4,890	5,500	*	5,000
Disk storage	47,000	45,000	*	47,000
Magnetic tape unit	11,000	10,500	*	11,000
CRT terminals	32,000	36,000	16,000	16,000
Modems and communications	2,000	3,000	4,500	4,000
OCR scanners	6,000	6,100	8,000	6,100
Software	8,665	15,000	18,200	152,000
Site preparation	4,000	4,500	4,000	4,000
Totals	$157,255	$144,730	$259,700	$283,100

*Included in the CPU cost.

Chart G-3. Summary of Estimated Annual Operating Costs for 5 Years for the Alternative Circulation Systems

Cost Element	Existing System	Handy Dandy System	Ultimate Circulation System	Solve-All Circulation System	System Designed Locally
Salaries and wages	$296,532	$180,187	$180,187	$180,187	$180,187
Supplies	6,770	21,029	21,029	21,029	23,400
Hardware maintenance	N/A	54,680	57,938	82,100	43,580
Software maintenance	N/A	11,120	8,620	15,000	10,000
Contractual services	42,500	42,500	42,500	44,200	38,200
Miscellaneous	4,000	4,000	4,000	6,200	3,800
Totals	$349,802	$313,516	$314,274	$348,716	$299,167

Chart G-4. The Decision Chart for Selecting the Best System

Decision Element	Existing System	Handy Dandy System	Ultimate Circulation System	Solve-All Circulation System	System Designed Locally
Meets all requirements set by the library	No	No	Yes	No	Yes
Estimated development costs	N/A	$157,255	$144,730	$259,700	$283,100
Annual operating costs for 5 years	$349,802	313,516	314,274	348,716	299,167
Combined developmental and operating costs	$349,802	$470,771	$459,004	$608,416	$582,267

Appendix H
Sample Parts of a Design
Report for a Circulation System

PURPOSE OF THE SYSTEM

The purpose of the circulation system is to provide a means by which registered borrowers can borrow materials from the library's collections and provide accountability for their return.

SUBSYSTEMS OF THE SYSTEM

The system will require several subsystems:

1. Borrower registration.
2. Charge.
3. Discharge
4. Renewals.
5. Holds.
6. Overdues.
7. Statistics.
8. Other notices and reports.

CHARGE FUNCTION

This subsystem will provide a means by which borrowers may charge out library materials for designated periods of time and by which to maintain records of these loan transactions. Specifically, the subsystem must:

1. Provide for borrower cards to be optically scanned as a means of entering their identification numbers into the system.
2. Accept borrower identification numbers entered on the keyboard in case cards are not available.

3. Check borrower records in the borrower file to make certain fines are not owed or items are not overdue and notify the operator with both audible and visual signals in either case.
4. Check the loan period code for items to be circulated in the bibliographic file and compute the dates due.
5. Add borrower identification numbers, the dates lent, and the dates due to records in the bibliographic file.
6. Print date-due slips for borrowers as reminders of loans.
7. Charge out additional items to the same borrower without having to rescan borrower cards.
8. Have the capability of informing borrowers of all materials charged to their records.

FILE REQUIREMENTS

The circulation system will require access to 2 online files: the borrower file and the bibliographic file.

Borrower File. The borrower file will contain a record for each registered borrower and will contain the following fields in each record:

Tag 01: Borrower number . . . . Fixed length (5 numeric)
Tag 02: Borrower name . . . . Variable length
Tag 03: Street address . . . . Variable length
Tag 04: City . . . . Variable length
Tag 05: State . . . . Fixed length (2 alpha)
Tag 06: ZIP code . . . . Fixed length (5 numeric)
Tag 07: Telephone number . . . . Fixed length (7 numeric)
Tag 08: Date record entered . . . . Fixed length (5 numeric)
Tag 09: Date record last used . . . . Fixed length (5 numeric)
Tag 10: Items overdue over 30 days . . . Fixed length (2 numeric)
Tag 11: Fines owed . . . . Fixed length (5 numeric)
Tag 12: Renewal notice sent code . . . . . Fixed length (1 numeric)

A total of approximately 120 characters/bytes of storage will be required per record.

Bibliographic File. The bibliographic file will contain a record for all materials received and cataloged, missing or lost, and withdrawn. Records of circulation transactions will be appended to these bibliographic records. Each record will contain the following fields:

Tag 01: Accession number . . . . Fixed length (6 numeric)
Tag 02: Type of material code . . . . Fixed length (1 numeric)

Tag 03: Library unit .... Fixed length (2 numeric)
Tag 04: Volume number .... Fixed length (2 numeric)
Tag 05: Author..................... Variable length
Tag 06: Title .... Variable length
Tag 07: Edition .... Variable length
Tag 08: Publisher.................. Variable length
Tag 09: Publication date .... Variable length
Tag 10: Pagination................. Variable length
Tag 11: Illustration statement .... Variable length
Tag 12: Special class code .... Fixed length (1 alpha)
Tag 13: Class number .... Variable length
Tag 14: Author number............. Fixed length (1 alpha)
Tag 15: Subject headings .... Variable length
        (repeated up to 3 times per title as needed)
Tag 16: Price .... Fixed length (4 numeric)
Tag 17: Date received .... Fixed length (5 numeric)
Tag 18: Date missing or lost......... Fixed length (5 numeric)
Tag 19: Loan period .... Fixed length (1 numeric)
Tag 20: Date lent.................. Fixed length (5 numeric)
Tag 21: Date due.................. Fixed length (5 numeric)
Tag 22: Borrower number........... Fixed length (5 numeric)
Tag 23: Overdues sent.............. Fixed length (1 numeric)
Tag 24: Date last overdue sent .... Fixed length (5 numeric)
Tag 25: Times circulated............ Fixed length (2 numeric)
Tag 26: Record status code.......... Fixed length (1 numeric)

A total of approximately 400 characters/bytes of storage will be required per record. Records will be created in this file automatically as materials are released from the acquisitions system.

CHECK OUT AN ITEM ROUTINE

This routine will be used to check out one or more items to a borrower via either the optical scanner or the manual keyboard. The system also will check to determine if the borrower is valid and/or delinquent and will enable variable due dates to be entered. The optical scanner terminals will be in this mode automatically at all times. To use other routines, the operator must exit from this routine and enter another. Flowcharts for the process of checking out items to borrowers follow. Screen messages the operator will see are also shown.

Chart H-1. Decision Flowchart: Check Out an Item Routine

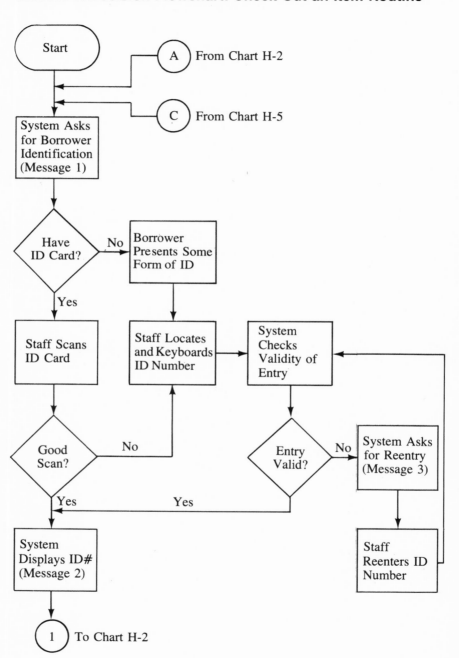

Chart H-2. Decision Flowchart (cont'd)

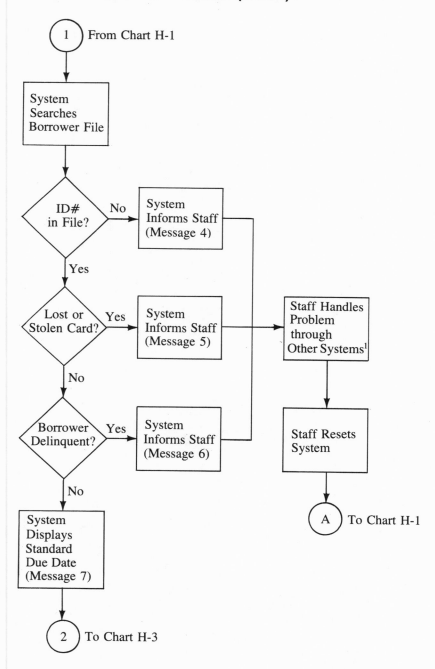

Chart H-3. Decision Flowchart (cont'd)

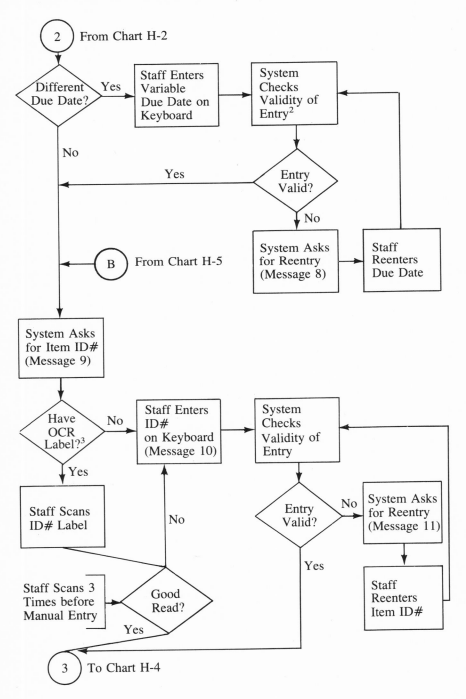

Chart H-4. Decision Flowchart (cont'd)

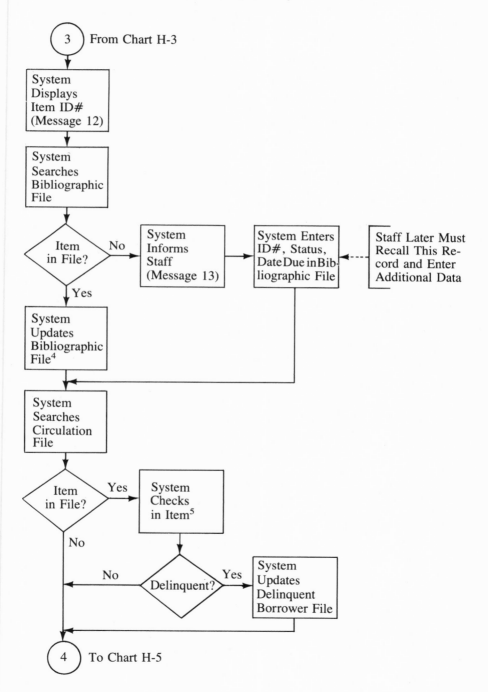

Chart H-5. Decision Flowchart (cont'd)

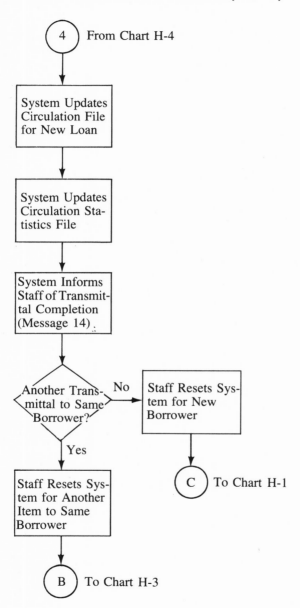

Chart H-6. System Messages

	1–10	11–20	21–30	31–40	41–50	51–60	61–70	71–80
01								
02								
03	ENTER BORROWER ID#:						(MESSAGE 1)	
04	ENTER BORROWER I.D#: XXXXXX						(MESSAGE 2)	
05	INVALID ENTRY... ENTER AGAIN. BORROWER I.D#:						(MESSAGE 3)	
06	BORROWER ID# NOT ON FILE...						(MESSAGE 4)	
07	ID# REPORTED LOST OR STOLEN.						(MESSAGE 5)	
08	BORROWER IS DELINQUENT						(MESSAGE 6)	
09	ITEM DUE:						(MESSAGE 7)	
10	INVALID ENTRY. ENTER AGAIN. ITEM DUE:						(MESSAGE 8)	
11	ENTER ITEM ID#:						(MESSAGE 9)	
12	ENTER ITEM ID#: XXXXXX						(MESSAGE 10)	
13	INVALID ENTRY.. ENTER AGAIN. ITEM ID#:						(MESSAGE 11)	
14	ENTER ITEM ID#: XXXXXX						(MESSAGE 12)	
15	ITEM NOT ON FILE						(MESSAGE 13)	
16	ITEM XXXXXX CHECKED OUT TO BORROWER XXXXXX DUE XXXXXX						(MESSAGE 14)	
17								
18								
19								
20								
21								
22								
23								
24								

Notes

1. When a borrower's ID number is not in the file or a card has been reported lost or stolen or a borrower is delinquent, the operator should exit from the regular optical scan terminal system and go to the special CRT/keyboard to solve the problems. In this manner, normal circulation transactions can continue without monopolizing the scanning terminals.

2. The system will have to be programmed to recognize a valid due date. The system should consider invalid any due date entered which is not all numeric or which is longer than 6 characters in length. The format "MMYYDD" can be used; in this way, the 12 months of the year, the 31 possible days of a month, and the current year can be programmed into the system and checks can easily be made by the system.

3. Until all items have scannable labels, a method of adding them during the circulation process should be worked out. Probably the simplest method is to have a number of gummed labels at the circulation desk; the staff can peel the next number off, stick one copy on the item to be circulation and one on the old book card (or other appropriate identification). The label on the item can be scanned and the borrower sent on her or his way. Later, information from the book card with the label attached can be entered into the bibliographic file. A procedure for items without book cards will have to be worked out.

4. That is, the system will change the status of the item to "In Circulation" and add the current date or perhaps the date-due or perhaps both.

5. This step will be necessary only when an item is returned to the shelves without being discharged first.

Appendix I
A Checklist of Hardware, Software, and Other Items for Typical Computer-Based Systems

HARDWARE FOR AN IN-HOUSE COMPUTER SYSTEM

1. The central processing unit (CPU) and cabinet.
2. Magnetic disk drive(s) and controller(s).
3. Magnetic tape drive(s) and controller(s).
4. Operator's console.
5. Line or serial printer(s).
6. Data communications controller(s) or line multiplexor(s).
7. Data communications modem(s).
8. Visual display terminal(s).

HARDWARE FOR REMOTE TERMINAL STATIONS

1. Visual display terminal(s).
2. OCR or bar code wand scanner(s) and controller(s).
3. Slave printer(s).
4. Data cassette deck(s) for system backup.
5. Data communications modem(s).
6. Line or serial printer(s).

SOFTWARE

1. Operating system (OS).
2. Language compiler (COBOL, FORTRAN, etc.).
3. Data base maintenance system.
4. Utilities (merging, sorting, etc.).
5. Program(s) for each application.

MANUFACTURER AND VENDOR ASSISTANCE

1. Hardware installation and testing (usually free with purchase or lease of hardware).
2. Software installation and testing (usually free with purchase or lease of software).
3. Hardware maintenance after installation and testing.
4. Software maintenance after installation and testing.
5. Hardware technical and operating manuals and their updates (sometimes free with purchase or lease of hardware).
6. Software technical and operating manuals and their updates (sometimes free with purchase or lease of software).
7. Provision of staff orientation and training.

Appendix J
A Sample RFP for a Turnkey Circulation System

INTRODUCTION

Purpose and Scope. The purpose of this request for proposal (RFP) is to request bids to supply an automated circulation system to be installed in the Mount Olympus Memorial Library. It is the intent of the library to purchase the system and a multiyear maintenance agreement from the successful bidder. The system bid by respondents to this RFP must meet or exceed all requirements set forth in this document to satisfy the anticipated needs of the library. Delivery of equipment, software, and related documentation will be required 120 days after the award of a contract to the successful bidder.

Background Information. Mount Olympus Memorial Library is located on beautiful Mount Olympus and provides library services to its 500,000 users from a central research library of 800,000 volumes, 5 suburban branches, and 10 bookmobiles for outlying areas. The library has a highly qualified staff of librarians, information specialists, and others to provide a full range of services supporting the research and recreational needs of its users.

The library began studying automation of its services 5 years ago and has developed a long-range plan for all projects to develop computer-based systems. The purpose of this particular project is to select, develop, and install an automated circulation system for the library. Growing pressures of an expanding and increasingly complex information base; of demands for new and sophisticated approaches to information access and dissemination; and of rising costs are forcing the library to take advantage of appropriate technological advancements within the information and data processing industry to address these and other problems. The hardware and software products that are explicitly identified within this RFP are intended to alleviate somewhat these and other problems in the circulation and, eventually, other functions of the library.

The Current System. The existing circulation system in the library is a manual Gaylord charging system. Data for unique identification of items to be circulated are typed on cards placed in pockets inside materials. Eligible borrowers are issued library cards bearing unique numbers embossed in metal tags affixed to the cards. When a borrower wishes to check out an item, her or his library card and the book card are inserted into the charging machine, which imprints both the date-due and the borrower number onto the book card. The date-due is stamped on a slip in the material as a reminder of the loan. The book card then is filed manually by date-due in a circulation file. As items are returned, the book cards are pulled from the circulation file and placed back in the pockets of the materials. Overdues are handled by checking the file for unreturned materials past the date-due.

Borrower's names and addresses are located by checking a list arranged by card number, and overdue notices are typed manually on postcards and mailed. The hold function is accomplished by clipping a note to the book card in the circulation file. All filing, overdue notice and list preparation, file searching, record retrieval, and counting of statistics must be done manually; no managerial reports such as tabulations of individual material usage can be compiled due to lack of time required for the tasks. The system is labor-intensive; as service demands increase, more staff must be added to handle the additional work load if the quality of service is not to deteriorate.

The Planned System. In the planned system, a number of circulation stations, each consisting of a CRT display terminal and an optical scanner, will be connected online to the computer located in the library. A borrower wishing to check out materials will go to a circulation station and present the material and her or his identification badge to the attendant. After the badge has been read, the system automatically will check the borrower file for clearance to loan materials to the borrower. Then the scanner will be passed over a machine-readable label containing a unique identifier on the material to be checked out; information encoded in the label will be read and recorded automatically in a circulation file as being on loan to the borrower. The date-due will be automatically printed on a slip which will be given to the borrower.

As items are returned from circulation, the scanner will be passed again over the labels, with the system in a discharge mode, and the records of the loans will be removed from the circulation file. The system automatically will calculate and record any charges for overdue materials. Any holds or personal reserves previously placed in a hold file will be detected and notices printed informing a waiting borrower of the availability of the materials. Other programs will be provided for logging transactions for file recovery; for searching and displaying individual borrower and circulation records; for entering, modifying, and deleting records; and for recording statistics. A medium-speed printer will be used to print overdue, fine, and availability notices; lists of overdues; and statistical and other managerial reports.

GENERAL GROUND RULES FOR THE RFP

<u>Vendor Contact Person</u>. After receipt of this RFP, vendors will be given an opportunity to consult, upon request, with the library staff. Appointments to clarify any items pertaining to the RFP should be made through:

> David McZeus, Project Manager
> Mount Olympus Memorial Library
> 123 Titan Way
> Mount Olympus 12345
> Telephone (123) 456-7890.

Any questions requiring responses affecting the bid and related responses that arise during the preparation of the vendor's response to the RFP should be directed in writing to the library. Questions may be submitted up to 2 weeks prior to bid opening. Only information supplied by the library in writing or in this RFP should be used in preparing vendor responses. All contacts that a vendor may have had before or after receipt of this RFP with any individuals, employees, or representatives of the library, or any information that may have been read in any news media or seen or heard on any communication facility regarding the acquisition of an automated circulation system by the library should be disregarded in preparing responses.

<u>Timetable</u>. The expected sequence of events to be followed is listed in the schedule below.

RFP distributed to bidders . . . . September 1, 19__.
Bidder inquiries and requests for briefings, interviews,
or demonstrations accepted until 4:30 p.m. . . . . October 1, 19__.
Delivery of bids due in the library by 4:30 p.m. . . . . October 15, 19__.
Bids opened at 9:00 a.m. . . . . October 16, 19__.
Contract will be awarded . . . . November 15, 19__.
Delivery and installation of equipment, software, and
documentation expected. . . . . March 15, 19__.

<u>Delivery of Bids</u>. Four copies of a vendor's bids should be delivered to the library at the place, time, and date shown on the invitation to bid. All bids and supporting documentation submitted become public property at the time of bid opening. At its option, a vendor may submit more than one

bid. If a vendor elects to do so, it is requested to identify each bid as either primary or alternate. Only one primary bid will be accepted. Each bid submitted, 'whether primary or alternate, should follow the instructions to vendors for submitting responses described in this RFP. For alternative bids, a vendor may refer by name and number to specific sections or paragraphs in the primary bid, rather than reproduce information that has not changed. Information in the primary bid that is referenced in the alternate bid will be considered as an integral part of the alternate bid for evaluation and contractual purposes.

Demonstration of System. At the option of the library, a vendor may be required to demonstrate the operation of the equipment and software being bid. The location of this demonstration will be at a site mutually agreeable to the library and the vendor(s). Vendors must demonstrate their proposed equipment within 10 days of receipt of written notice from the library.

The intent of a demonstration is to assure the library of the ability of a vendor's bid items to meet the requirements specified in this RFP. The equipment configuration and software demonstrated must be identical to that proposed for installation in the library. The circulation system used to run the demonstration must be dedicated to this demonstration. The sample system files listed below must be stored on magnetic disk and available for the demonstration:

1. Title.
2. Copy or item.
3. Borrower.
4. Statistics.

At least one copy of the user documentation must be provided for use and consultation during the demonstration. The demonstration will be conducted in 3 parts:

1. A demonstration that records in each of the files above can be created, altered, and deleted, then displayed.
2. A demonstration that each of the following functions can be performed by the system:
   a. Checkout of items.
   b. Discharge of items.
   c. Renewal of items.
   d. Placement of holds on items and titles.
   e. Computation, recording, payment, adjustment, and deletion of fines.

3. A demonstration that each of the following notices and reports can be prepared and printed in paper form:
   a. First, second, and third overdue notices.
   b. Fines notices.
   c. Availability notices.
   d. Statistical report.
   e. List of borrowers by name, by identification number, and by census tract.

For a further explanation of each, refer to the library's requirements detailed in this RFP. The library will not be liable for any expenses incurred by the vendor or his representatives as a result of a demonstration.

Contractual Expectations. A copy of the complete contract for this procurement of equipment, software, and other items is available from the library. Each vendor interested in bidding is requested to obtain a copy or request that one be mailed to them. A vendor may agree to this contract as written, take exception to any paragraph and suggest substitute wording, and/or suggest additional clauses. However, vendors must not offer changes that conflict with the mandatory requirements of this RFP.

Each vendor is required to identify specifically any paragraph it desires to change and to submit the recommended changes as a part of its response or to add additional paragraphs as an "Addendum for Extraordinary Terms and Conditions." The library, as a part of the evaluation procedure, will evaluate each suggested change and either reject the change or place a penalty figure in the evaluation document to correspond to the value the suggested change has in relation to the expressed needs of the library. Each vendor may also elect to charge an additional amount in consideration for the acceptance of any paragraph or section of the proposed contract. If the vendor wishes to specify a charge for any items, it should identify the item and specify the amount of the charge.

A performance bond of 10 percent of the total bid, in a form acceptable to the library, will be required for the full term of the purchase order. It should be understood clearly that the terms and requirements contained in this RFP, and a bidder's responses to this request for proposal both shall be considered a part of the contract. Delivery of all items must be made, and all items must be installed and in working order, within 120 days after the contract is accepted. Prices for system components include unrestricted use by the library.

Method of Financing. It is the intent of the library to procure under this RFP, using a method of financing whereby 20 percent of the system's cost will be paid down, with the balance to be paid in 5 equal or approx-imately equal annual installment payments, with the library receiving title to the equipment when fully paid out. Vendors may, however, bid any other method of financing, so long as the library will receive title when all required payments have been made. The library reserves the right to choose any financing method offered in which the total cost to it will be less than the cost would be under the full pay-out lease or installment financing method.

Time Period. Prices and payments quoted for hardware and software must be firm for the full term of the purchase order. Maximum percentage cost escalation factors compounded by fiscal year may be bid for software and hardware maintenance. Potential price escalation factors will be applied in full by the library during bid evaluation and should be entered as such on the price schedules. All price sheets shown in the appendix to this RFP must be completed and returned with a bid.

Annual Payments. Bidders are requested to bid monthly payments for any recurring costs. Annual payments may be bid. If both monthly and annual payments are bid, any resulting savings to the library will be considered in the bid evaluation. Annual payments, if elected to be used by the library, will be paid as follows: the first payment will be paid with any applicable down payment the library offers to make; this first payment will be equal to an annual, prorated share of the months remaining in the calendar year of the total amount of the bid, less the down payment, and will be paid in the month following the month of acceptance. Lump-sum payments for subsequent fiscal years will be made in September. All payments covering a full fiscal year must be approximately equal. Separate price sheets should be completed for monthly and annual payments.

Buy-Out Price. Bidders are required to quote a buy-out price effective each September of the contract period. Bidders are required to offer a financing plan that includes the right of the library to accelerate payments as of any September 1 during the term of the purchase order. Any such payment acceleration plan must indicate clearly a method for calculating the savings available to the library as a result of a prepayment and must provide a method for recalculation of the remaining approximately even payments to be made.

Title to Hardware and Software. Although the library expects clear title to hardware to be delivered upon final payment, bidders may or may not deliver title to software. If a bidder retains title to software, a full-use software license must be provided to the library and must be effective for the full term of the contract and be extended to the library or subsequent users for as long as the hardware is usable. It is the intent of this specification to ensure availability of software license, with or without bidder-supplied support, for software other than system control software. Such additional software shall be available via vendor software license (not necessarily the bidding vendor), presuming a proper performance by the licensee, at the bid price, terms, and conditions throughout the term of this contract and at the same prices, terms, and conditions that are offered to customers similar in class to the users of the hardware in this transaction, from the end of the contract term until the hardware is no longer usable.

Evaluation of Bids. Bids will be evaluated by a team of librarians and data processing specialists, who will select the proposal offering the best and lowest bid conforming to specifications outlined in this RFP. The library reserves the right to contact a bidder for clarification of information submitted, to contact current users of equipment or software bid, and to use other sources for obtaining information regarding the hardware, software, or vendor that is deemed appropriate and would assist in the evaluation. In evaluating the bids, the library reserves the right to:

1. Accept or reject all or any part of any bid, waive minor technicalities, and award the bid to best serve the interests of the library.
2. Use, without limitations, any or all of the ideas from all bids submitted.
3. Adopt any part or all of a bid in selecting the optimum system, if it is judged in the best interests of the library.

If a bid does not include, in the library's opinion, the correct amount or type of hardware, including memory, software, maintenance, training, or other needed items, sufficient items may be priced and included in the evaluation at unit prices, if listed in the bid; otherwise, such items will be priced and included at the vendor or manufacturer's current list prices, with terms and conditions published in a price list effective at bid opening date and available for review by the library. Application of such amounts to the evaluation is for the purpose of retaining as viable those bids which the library considers not meeting specifications in a minor way, but which otherwise are worthy of further consideration. Such decisions will be made by the library.

SPECIFICATIONS AND REQUIREMENTS

Vendors should remove and reproduce this section, then answer each question and complete the appropriate blanks as a part of their bid response. The term "reference" used below refers to the vendor's manual(s) or performance specifications accompanying the bid and page(s) where answers to questions can be confirmed; manuals so referenced must accompany the bid.

I. Mandatory Hardware Requirements

The equipment configuration desired in this installation is shown in Appendix J-1.

A. Central Processing Unit

1. Does the central processing unit bid for initial installation have sufficient features to perform the initial workloads described in Appendix J-2 for the full purchase order term?
YES _____ NO _____ REFERENCE _____

2. Can the CPU bid for initial installation be expanded, by adding processor features to speed up the CPU, by adding multiple CPUs, or by other methods such as adding additional memory, to perform the expanded workloads shown in the workload tables? (*Note:* Bid must specifically show how expansion will be accomplished to meet this requirement.)
YES _____ NO _____ REFERENCE _____

3. Are the total amount and speed of real memory bid for initial installation sufficient to provide at least 128K bytes (8-bit bytes or equivalent) for user-written programs and to provide sufficient additional memory for all other software necessary to be resident in real memory in order to meet the performance and response time specifications and handle workload requirements that are shown in Appendix J-2?
YES _____ NO _____ REFERENCE _____

4. Can real memory be expanded to a minimum of 256K bytes (8-bit bytes or equivalent) for user-written programs to accommodate the expanded workloads as expressed in this RFP and continue to meet the performance and response time specifications listed in this RFP?
YES _____ NO _____ REFERENCE _____

5. Does the bid submitted for initial installation include all the required control and interface equipment necessary to integrate the central processing unit and the peripherals into a functional system initially and over the purchase order term?
YES _____ NO _____ REFERENCE _____

6. Does the central processing unit and/or attached unit(s) (such as I/O channels) bid for initial installation provide input/output paths of sufficient speed and capacity to allow concurrent operation of the peripherals, at or near rated speeds and to meet the performance and response requirements included in this RFP?
YES _____ NO _____ REFERENCE _____

7. Can the initially installed capabilities of the CPU either provide for similar operation of expansion peripherals described in this RFP, or

does the system bid have input/output path(s) expansion capability sufficient to handle expanded peripherals described in this RFP?
YES ____ NO ____ REFERENCE _____

B. System or Operator Console
Does the system bid for initial installation have a console which can be used for communication, at a speed of at least 30 cps, between the operator or maintenance engineer and the computer and for initiation and control of batch programs?
YES ____ NO ____ REFERENCE _____

C. Magnetic Disk Storage
1. Does the system bid for initial installation include at least one removable pack spindle of magnetic disk storage and the necessary associated controller(s) to provide at least 192 million bytes (8-bit or equivalent) available for user data files with a minimum data transfer rate of 250K characters per second and with a maximum average access time, including latency, of 42.5 milliseconds?
YES ____ NO ____ REFERENCE _____
2. Is the system expandable to a minimum of 300 million bytes (8-bit or equivalent) available for user data files on compatible and/or identical disk drives without additional controllers?
YES ____ NO ____ REFERENCE _____

D. Magnetic Tape
Does the system bid include one magnetic tape drive and required controller, 9-track, 800 or 1600 BPI, capable of reading and writing, with read-after-write check, industry-compatible, half-inch magnetic tape in ASCII format at a minimum speed of 20–25 inches per second?
YES ____ NO ____ REFERENCE _____

E. Printer
1. Does the system bid for initial installation include a printer and any necessary controller with 132 print positions, print spacing of 10 characters per inch horizontally and 6 lines per inch vertically, 4-inch to 14⅞-inches horizontal paper adjustment, first print position adjustable, top-of-forms sensing, manual forms eject, pin-fed continuous forms tractor feed, programmed carriage control, high-quality print on at least 4-part paper, rated speed of not less than 160 characters per second when printing full 132-character lines; and standard 64 ASCII character set?
YES ____ NO ____ REFERENCE _____
2. Does the print set bid have as a minimum the characters shown below and is a sample of print quality (of the printer bid) on

multipart paper (minimum of 4-part) included with the vendor's bid response?

1 2 3 4 5 6 7 8 9 0 A B C D E F G H I J K L M N O P Q R S T U V W X Y Z [ ] @ # $ % ¢ & * ( ) — - + = " ' ; : , . ? /

YES _____ NO _____ REFERENCE _____

F. Communications Control

1. Does the system bid for initial installation include all communications control hardware sufficient in capacity and configured to process the communications input and output workload covered by the purchase order term and within the performance requirements specified in Appendix J-2?
YES _____ NO _____ REFERENCE _____

2. Does the communications control hardware include proper interface and support for the devices shown in the equipment configuration in Appendix J-1?
YES _____ NO _____ REFERENCE _____

G. CRT Terminals

1. Does the CRT display terminals bid have a minimum display capacity of 1,920 characters with a screen display image of at least 24 displayable lines vertical and with 80 characters horizontal on each line?
YES _____ NO _____ REFERENCE _____

2. Does the display area (usable screen) of the CRT display terminal have a diagonal measurement of at least 12 inches?
YES _____ NO _____ REFERENCE _____

3. Does the CRT display terminal's display provide a nondestructible, single-character, addressable cursor?
YES _____ NO _____ REFERENCE _____

4. Does the CRT display terminal have an audible alarm?
YES _____ NO _____ REFERENCE _____

5. Does the CRT terminal's display use American English block-style for uppercase alphabetic and numeric characters?
YES _____ NO _____ REFERENCE _____

6. Does the resolution of the CRT terminal's display equal or exceed that obtainable with a dot matrix of 5 dots wide by 7 dots high?
YES _____ NO _____ REFERENCE _____

7. Does the CRT terminal's cursor control allow the operator to maneuver the cursor up, down, left, right, home, and return?
YES _____ NO _____ REFERENCE _____

8. Is the CRT display terminal capable of interfacing (hard-wired) with the scanning wands below or RS-232C compatible with the CPU above?
   YES _____ NO _____ REFERENCE _____
9. Will the CRT terminal operate properly at standard data transmission rates from 300 to 9600 bps using teletypewriter communications line protocol?
   YES _____ NO _____ REFERENCE _____

H. Optical Scanning Wands and Terminal Units

Does the system bid include 10 optical scanning wands and necessary hardware, cables, and control units, installed according to the workload tables in Appendix J-2, with hand-held wand scanners with flexible cords at least 36 inches in length (unflexed), capable of reading the Universal Product Code (UPC), the 2-out-of-5 code, or OCR labels, and capable of interfacing (hard-wired) with the CRT display terminals described above, or RS-232C compatible with the CPU described also above?
YES _____ NO _____ REFERENCE _____

II. Mandatory System Software Requirements

The vendor must identify specifically the software product or products being bid to meet the specifications.

A. General

1. Will the vendor supply one set of operator's manuals with each item of equipment delivered? (*Note:* If there is a charge for these manuals, indicate cost in bid.)
   YES _____ NO _____ REFERENCE _____
2. Is a set of software for initial installation bid with sufficient capabilities in at least the functions listed below to be used with the mandatory hardware to accomplish the workloads as described in the workload tables in Appendix J-2 for the entire purchase order term within the performance and response times specified in this RFP?
   YES _____ NO _____ REFERENCE _____

B. Operating System

1. Does the operating system bid provide for efficient utilization of the CPU, as well as all input/output devices, by scheduling jobs in such a way that their I/O and processing time requirements are balanced?
   YES _____ NO _____ REFERENCE _____
2. Does the operating system bid provide for automatic scheduling and loading of programs into memory?
   YES _____ NO _____ REFERENCE _____

3. Does the operating system bid provide for the processing of jobs in accordance with established priorities, by scheduling jobs, overlapping jobs requiring operator action with jobs requiring no operator action, and issuing messages to the operator?
   YES ____ NO ____ REFERENCE _____

4. Does the operating system bid provide for the queuing and dispatching of I/O results in order to provide multitask I/O support?
   YES ____ NO ____ REFERENCE _____

5. Does the operating system bid provide a means of exercising control after a program is interrupted, saving the status of the interrupted program, and determining the routine required to process the interrupt condition?
   YES ____ NO ____ REFERENCE _____

6. Does the operating system bid include standard error handling routines which will assure that operator intervention is kept to a minimum?
   YES ____ NO ____ REFERENCE _____

7. Does the operating system bid provide an interrupt-handling program that coordinates transfer of control between programs after an interrupt?
   YES ____ NO ____ REFERENCE _____

8. Does the operating system bid adjust to the addition of future peripheral equipment with only minor software changes?
   YES ____ NO ____ REFERENCE _____

9. Does the operating system bid provide for the receiving, processing, and dispatching of remote messages from the CRT terminals?
   YES ____ NO ____ REFERENCE _____

10. Does the operating system bid permit real-time programs to be executed in the foreground, while at least one batch program can be executed during leftover processing time in the background?
    YES ____ NO ____ REFERENCE _____

C. Utility Programs
   1. Is a sort/merge utility system bid that can support multidisk files, incorporate user-written processing before and after the sorting and/or merging process, be called into use by user-written statements in programs, be modified to handle files with various record formats, support up to 50-character key lengths, and use either disk or tape for input or output?
      YES ____ NO ____ REFERENCE _____

   2. Is a set of file conversion routines bid that can perform tape-to-disk conversion, disk-to-tape conversion, and disk duplication?
      YES ____ NO ____ REFERENCE _____

III. Mandatory Application Software Requirements

A. General

   1. Is a set of programs bid which will provide circulation control for library materials as described below and according to the workload tables in Appendix J-2?
YES ____ NO ____ REFERENCE _____

   2. Can the library alter or modify the programs without permission of the vendor?
YES ____ NO ____ REFERENCE _____

   3. Is documentation for the software bid provided which will enable the library to make modifications to the programs when necessary?
YES ____ NO ____ REFERENCE _____

B. Borrower Control Function

   1. Will the system provide for entry of data collected about borrowers during their registration?
YES ____ NO ____ REFERENCE _____

   2. Will the borrower file contain an identification number, name, address, city, state, ZIP code, telephone number, branch where registered, date of registration, date of last use, and number of items charged for each person registered?
YES ____ NO ____ REFERENCE _____

   3. Will the system allow records to be deleted from the borrower file for borrowers who do not renew their registrations after specified dates?
YES ____ NO ____ REFERENCE _____

   4. Will the system accept changes, additions, and deletions to any date in records in the borrower file from the terminals?
YES ____ NO ____ REFERENCE _____

   5. Will the system accommodate up to 15 library-designated user types?
YES ____ NO ____ REFERENCE _____

C. Charge Function

   1. Can materials be charged rapidly to borrowers, with response time of 3 seconds or less average per charge?
YES ____ NO ____ REFERENCE _____

   2. Can borrower identification cards be scanned optically as a means of entering the numbers?
YES ____ NO ____ REFERENCE _____

   3. Can borrower identification numbers also be entered manually on a keyboard?
YES ____ NO ____ REFERENCE _____

4. Does the system check whether borrowers are eligible to use the library, their borrowing privileges, and their status and alert the operator with both audible and visual prompts of blocks or other unusual circumstances?
YES _____ NO _____ REFERENCE _____

5. Does the system permit overriding of blocks when necessary?
YES _____ NO _____ REFERENCE _____

6. Does the system check the loan period codes for items to be circulated and automatically compute the dates due?
YES _____ NO _____ REFERENCE _____

7. Does the system permit the overriding of standard loan periods and settings of different loan periods when necessary?
YES _____ NO _____ REFERENCE _____

8. Does the system print date-due slips for borrowers?
YES _____ NO _____ REFERENCE _____

9. Can additional items be charged to the same borrower without having to rescan the identification card?
YES _____ NO _____ REFERENCE _____

10. Does the system allow checkout when necessary of items which do not normally circulate?
YES _____ NO _____ REFERENCE _____

11. Can materials be checked out to library departments, offices, or other library-designated units?
YES _____ NO _____ REFERENCE _____

12. Will the system disregard holidays in computing dates due?
YES _____ NO _____ REFERENCE _____

D. Discharge Function

1. Does the system provide for rapid and accurate discharging of materials returned by borrowers, with response times of 3 seconds or less per discharge?
YES _____ NO _____ REFERENCE _____

2. Does the system trap during the discharge process those items which are overdue or with holds placed against them?
YES _____ NO _____ REFERENCE _____

3. Can the system compute and record fines owed if items are overdue and notify the operator with both audible and visual prompts when such situations occur?
YES _____ NO _____ REFERENCE _____

4. Will the system use library-specified assessment rates for the different types of borrowers when computing fines?
YES _____ NO _____ REFERENCE _____

5. Will the system accept and record fines paid on the spot?
YES _____ NO _____ REFERENCE _____

6. Will the system accept partial payment of fines owed?
YES _____ NO _____ REFERENCE _____

7. Will the system automatically increase the counter in bibliographic records for the number of times items have circulated?
YES _____ NO _____ REFERENCE _____

8. Will the system erase borrower identification numbers from the bibliographic and/or circulation files when items have been discharged, to preserve privacy of the individual?
YES _____ NO _____ REFERENCE _____

9. When items being discharged must be returned to locations outside the library, will the system alert the operator with both audible and visual signals and indicate the branch designations?
YES _____ NO _____ REFERENCE _____

E. Renewals
1. Will the system complete renewals with or without borrower's cards and with or without the physical items in hand?
YES _____ NO _____ REFERENCE _____

2. Will the system check for reserves or holds on items and notify the operator if any exist?
YES _____ NO _____ REFERENCE _____

3. Will the system follow all other routines or requirements for charges when renewing loans of materials?
YES _____ NO _____ REFERENCE _____

F. Holds Function
1. Will the system accept holds on items in circulation?
YES _____ NO _____ REFERENCE _____

2. Will the system retain holds on items in the order in which they are placed by borrowers?
YES _____ NO _____ REFERENCE _____

3. Will the system allow holds to be changed or canceled upon request of borrowers?
YES _____ NO _____ REFERENCE _____

4. Will the system allow hold queues to be overridden by the staff when necessary?
YES _____ NO _____ REFERENCE _____

5. Can holds be placed on either individual copies or all copies of a title?
YES _____ NO _____ REFERENCE _____

G. The Bibliographic File

1. Can bibliographic and item records be added, changed, or deleted?
YES ____ NO ____ REFERENCE _____

2. Will the system accept either full or partial records in the MARC II format?
YES ____ NO ____ REFERENCE _____

3. Does the item record contain item/copy identification number, location, cost, and times the item/copy has circulated?
YES ____ NO ____ REFERENCE _____

4. Will the system interface with OCLC without additional hardware?
YES ____ NO ____ REFERENCE _____

5. Does the system have authority files for main entries and subject headings?
YES ____ NO ____ REFERENCE _____

6. Will the system update the bibliographic file automatically when new or updated main entries or subject headings are added to the authority files?
YES ____ NO ____ REFERENCE _____

H. Inquiry Function

1. Will the system allow rapid determination of titles in the bibliographic file and their locations?
YES ____ NO ____ REFERENCE _____

2. Does the system have a response time of 6 seconds or less for author, title, or patron inquiries, and 10 seconds or less for subject, call number, LC card number, and ISSN/ISBN?
YES ____ NO ____ REFERENCE _____

3. Can the files be searched by author, title, subject, call number, LC card number, ISBN/ISSN, and patron name?
YES ____ NO ____ REFERENCE _____

4. Will the system display items on loan to borrowers during a borrower search?
YES ____ NO ____ REFERENCE _____

5. Will the system display a brief listing of all matches to a search argument if more than one match is found, thus enabling the operator to choose the correct one, and ''no postings'' if no matches are found?
YES ____ NO ____ REFERENCE _____

I. Notices and Reports

1. Will the system compile and print first, second, and third overdue notices upon demand?
YES ____ NO ____ REFERENCE _____

2. Will the system compile and print fine and availability notices upon demand?
YES _____ NO _____ REFERENCE _____

3. Will the system compile and print a report of all items having exceeded a library-designated number of holds?
YES _____ NO _____ REFERENCE _____

4. Will the system compile and print lists of borrowers by either name or ZIP code, materials on loan by units to other units, fines outstanding, lost and missing materials, and circulation statistics by borrower type and by branch or location?
YES _____ NO _____ REFERENCE _____

IV. Mandatory Staff Training Requirements

A. Has a list of all available courses (both at the library and vendor sites), including costs, been included with the bid?
YES _____ NO _____ REFERENCE _____

B. Does the vendor's bid include a training plan to cover necessary formal training for 5 members of the library staff, with follow-up training as necessary?
YES _____ NO _____ REFERENCE _____

C. Will the vendor's training result in the following competencies for 3 system operators and 2 library managers?

1. Ability to start up and shut down the system and to monitor and operate the system on a day-to-day basis.
YES _____ NO _____ REFERENCE _____

2. Ability to handle emergencies with the system which might arise from time to time before the vendor's maintenance staff can arrive.
YES _____ NO _____ REFERENCE _____

3. Ability to troubleshoot and solve simple problems with the system in lieu of calling the vendor's maintenance staff.
YES _____ NO _____ REFERENCE _____

D. Will the vendor supply a complete set of system documentation, including 5 detailed guides to use for each of the circulation functions?
YES _____ NO _____ REFERENCE _____

E. Will the vendor supply all revisions and enhancements to the above documentation for a period of 5 years from the date of installation?
YES _____ NO _____ REFERENCE _____

V. Mandatory Hardware Maintenance Requirements

A. General

    1. Does the vendor agree to keep all equipment delivered in good operating condition?
YES _____ NO _____ REFERENCE _____

    2. Is all hardware certified to qualify for full-coverage preventive and remedial maintenance?
YES _____ NO _____ REFERENCE _____

B. Preventive and Remedial Maintenance

    1. Is all-expense, flat-rate preventive and remedial hardware mainte-nance for the equipment bid, with the principal period of mainte-nance at the library from 8:00 a.m. to 5:00 p.m., Monday through Friday (library holidays excluded) with preventive maintenance, if required, performed outside the principal period of maintenance (8 a.m. through 5:00 p.m., Monday through Friday), at a time mutual-ly agreed upon by the vendor and the library? Prices for all-expense, flat-rate preventive and remedial hardware maintenance are guaran-teed to be firm until _____, with no more than _____ percent increase per year thereafter until the expiration date of the contract. (Vendor is to fill in the blanks above.)
YES __.__ NO _____ REFERENCE _____

    2. Is normal remedial maintenance contact by vendor maintenance personnel guaranteed to be within one hour after notification of need, with remedial work to begin within 4 hours after vendor contact, except in rare and unusual circumstances, through mutual-ly agreed to contacting procedures?
YES _____ NO _____ REFERENCE _____

    3. Is on-call, per call charge remedial maintenance available from 5 p.m. through 8 a.m., Monday through Sunday, library holidays excluded?
YES _____ NO _____ REFERENCE _____

    4. Will preventive maintenance, when required, be performed at a time mutually agreed upon by the library and the vendor? (Normal-ly, preventive maintenance will be performed other than during the prime shift.)
YES _____ NO _____ REFERENCE _____

    5. Do all maintenance personnel to be used have a minimum of one year's experience maintaining the equipment bid or will each have completed a comprehensive formal training program on the

appropriate bid items at least 3 months prior to the date of installation?
YES _____ NO _____ REFERENCE _____

6. Will vendor maintenance personnel provide library personnel with a brief written statement for each preventive or remedial maintenance activity performed, including date and time notified, date and time of arrival, type and model of machine, time spent for repair, description of malfunction, date and time equipment made operational, and initials of maintenance and library representatives?
YES _____ NO _____ REFERENCE _____

7. Will maintenance personnel provide library personnel with a short, signed statement of maintenance status after remedial maintenance has been unsuccessful after 4 hours, and every 4 hours thereafter that corrective efforts continue to be unsuccessful?
YES _____ NO _____ REFERENCE _____

C. Repair Parts
1. Will an adequate supply of repair parts be maintained locally to repair a minimum of 85 percent of all hardware failures during a calendar year?
YES _____ NO _____ REFERENCE _____

2. Can repair parts to meet the remaining 15 percent of hardware failures be made available within 24 hours, except under rare and unusual circumstances?
YES _____ NO _____ REFERENCE _____

VI. Mandatory Software Maintenance Requirements

A. Will the vendor provide a copy of technical and operator manual changes and other pertinent documentation changes and updates to the library? (*Note:* If there is a charge, such must be included in the bid.)
YES _____ NO _____ REFERENCE _____

B. Have prices for software support been quoted by the bidder? (Software support is defined as being any personnel, equipment use, manuals, or other documentation, travel expenses, or any other source of cost to the library necessary to take required action to correct software deficiency as determined by comparing actual software manuals and to furnish such materials and resources necessary to make the routine software improvements normally made available to such software users.)
YES _____ NO _____ REFERENCE _____

C. Do all software support personnel to be used have a minimum of one year's experience maintaining the software bid or will each have completed a comprehensive formal training program on the appropriate bid items at least 3 months prior to the date of installation?

YES ____ NO ____ REFERENCE _____

INSTRUCTIONS TO VENDORS FOR SUBMITTING RESPONSES

There is no intent to limit the contents of proposals, and these instructions permit the inclusion of any additional information a vendor deems pertinent. The library requests that the following section headings be used in vendor responses to this RFP and that these headings be arranged in the order listed below. Vendors should provide a table of contents and should label divider tabs with the wording underlined. Responses must be in sufficient detail to permit an understanding and comprehensive evaluation of a vendor's bid. A minimum of 4 copies of the bid and 2 complete sets of descriptive, operational manuals plus other documentation for each device bid and all its constituent parts must be furnished. Information should be sufficiently detailed to substantiate that products offered meet or exceed specifications. This latter documentation will be used in the evaluation of bids and may be returned, upon written request, except to the successful bidder whose documentation is to become the property of the library. Additionally, the successful bidder will be required to provide for one year one copy of any manual supplements and other pertinent documentation changes to the library.

Proposal Summary. The vendor should include a summary of its response, including a brief overview of the system bid and its features which should be particularly advantageous to the library.

Vendor Profile. The vendor may include brief facts as desired about the company. A copy of the vendor's latest annual report and/or Dun and Bradstreet's current rating must be included as part of this response, or other sources of financial information must be provided to permit the library to be satisfied with the financial stability of the vendor.

Response to Requirements. The vendor must complete the sections of mandatory requirements, extracted from this RFP, and submit them with the bid. A positive response to all requirements is necessary to insure total compatibility and compliance with all required specifications.

Vendor's User List. A description of the production and marketing history of the proposed equipment and software indicating a minimum of 3 users of the specific equipment and software must be included. Equipment in each case should have been in operation for at least 3 months at time of the bid opening. If possible, libraries or users serving libraries should be represented. The list of users must provide the name and address of the organization, the name, title, and telephone number of a responsible individual in the organization who may be contacted, the installed configuration and type of work being accomplished, and the date of installation. Representatives of the library, at their discretion, may call any of the firms listed or any other firms known to verify the performance of identical equipment bid, quality of maintenance, vendor responsiveness, etc. This information may be used in the bid evaluation.

Special Conditions. Any special conditions or terms that apply to a response to this RFP should be detailed.

Environmental and Physical Specifications. The environmental requirements (space, air conditioning, electrical power, security, and environmental impact) of the equipment bid should be detailed.

Cost Data. It is requested that each vendor present prices for hardware and software being bid in a form illustrated by the tables in the appendix to this RFP. Two copies of the current, published manufacturer's or vendor's price lists must also be submitted with each bid.

Supporting Data. Other relevant information supporting a bid, such as technical manuals, brochures, photographs, and schematics may be included as a part of a vendor's response to this RFP.

APPENDIX J-1
DESIRED EQUIPMENT CONFIGURATION

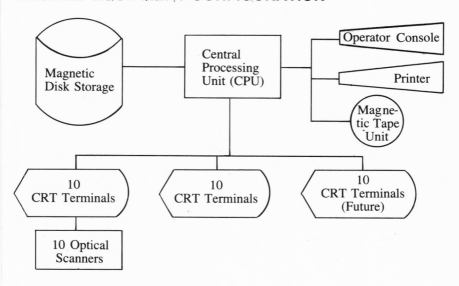

APPENDIX J-2
WORKLOAD TABLES

Listed and described below are the functional, file, and activity requirements of the circulation system desired. Several functions must be operational concurrently; most have more than one subfunction. While online transactions and file inquiries can be occurring simultaneously at different terminals, only one batch program will be executed at any one time.

Functions to Be Performed

The primary functions to be performed include the following:

Borrower Control
1. Borrower entry
2. Borrower modification
3. Borrower deletion
4. Statistics display
5. Statistics report printing

Circulation Control
1. Checkouts
2. Special checkouts
3. Renewals
4. Holds checkouts
5. Overdue notice printing
6. Overdue list printing
7. Delinquent list printing
8. Fines entry
9. Fines maintenance
10. Fines deletion
11. Fines notices
12. Statistics display
13. Statistics report printing

Holds
1. Hold entry
2. Hold modification
3. Hold deletion
4. Availability notice printing
5. Statistics display
6. Statistics report printing

Inventory Control
1. Title entry
2. Title modification
3. Title deletion
4. Item/copy entry
5. Item/copy modification
6. Item/copy deletion
7. Circulation count report printing
8. Statistics display
9. Statistics report printing

File Inquiries
1. By call number
2. By title
3. By item/copy number
4. By borrower number
5. By borrower name

Files to Be Maintained

The systems are heavily file oriented and file dependent. The following are the major files to be maintained.

1. Title File. A file of brief records of information describing the titles in the library's collections available for circulation. About 400,000 records of approximately 400 characters each.
2. Item File. A file of records of brief information describing each copy of a title owned by the library and available for circulation. About 700,000 records.
3. Borrower File. A file of patrons authorized to borrow materials from the library. About 20,000 records.
4. Fines File. A file of fines owed by delinquent borrowers. About 5,000 records at any one time.
5. Hold File. A file of records for personal holds or reserves placed on items in circulation. About 2,000 records at any one time.
6. Statistics File. A file of statistics accumulated during various transactions in the circulation system. About 200 statistical categories.

System Activities

1. Title records entered, modified, and deleted. About 50,000/year during initial file creation, then dropping to about 20,000/year.
2. Item/copy records entered, modified, and deleted. About 75,000/ year until the files are created, then dropping to about 30,000/ year.
3. Borrower records entered, modified, and deleted. About 13,000/ year.
4. Circulation checkout transactions. About 250,000/year.
5. Circulation check-in transactions. About 250,000/year.
6. Holds placed. About 2,000/year.
7. Fines transactions. About 10,000 transactions/year.

The number of file inquiries per year is unknown, since no statistics of the file use in the manual systems are available or possible to acquire. An estimate is that all files would be queried about 5,000,000 times a year. The batch programs will be run on demand, usually once a week or once a month, depending upon the type of program. As each transaction occurs, it will be recorded on magnetic tape or by some other acceptable backup method. Copies of all files will be retained on magnetic tape or disk and placed in another building for safekeeping. A time up to 10 seconds (expected average around 5 seconds) is desired for any response to a command by the computer.

SCHEDULE J-1. COST SUMMARY

Summary based on annual _____ monthly _____ payments (indicate which)

Bid Item	Amount Net 5 Years	Remarks
Hardware		
Hardware maintenance		
System software		
Application software		
Software maintenance		
Staff training		
Transportation		
Contract charges		
Documentation		
Miscellaneous costs		
Other (please list)		
Totals		

Note: To complete Schedule J-1, show total contract period costs to include all price escalation potentially required in bid.

SCHEDULE J-2. OUTRIGHT PURCHASE

Equipment Model Number	Description	Hardware Purchase	Maintenance Price* Monthly** Annual***	
		Totals		

*These rates are guaranteed to be firm until _____ with no more than _____ percent increase per year.
**Cost of maintenance if paid monthly.
***Cost of maintenance if paid annually.

Appendix K
A Sample Report of an Evaluation of Responses to the RFP in Appendix J

INTRODUCTION

This report summarizes the evaluation of responses received to the library's request for proposal (RFP) issued September 15, 19__, for an automated circulation system. Four vendors submitted bids to supply the system. The bids were reviewed and evaluated by a team of librarians and data processing specialists, who deemed the Handy Dandy System to be the best and lowest.

DECISION RULES FOR SELECTING THE BEST BID

Three decision rules were established for selecting the best bid by a vendor. The best bid was judged to be the one whose:

1. Hardware, software, staff training, and maintenance met all or most of the mandatory requirements set forth in the RFP.
2. Combined hardware, software, training, and maintenance costs were the lowest.
3. System, when demanded, could perform according to specifications outlined in the RFP.

VENDORS SUBMITTING RESPONSES TO THE RFP

Bids in response to the library's request for proposal were received from:

1. Handy Dandy Systems, Inc.
2. All-Right Systems, Inc.
3. Solve-All Company.
4. ABC Company.

THE EVALUATION TEAM

A team of 4 was selected to evaluate the bids received:

1. Grizelda Smith, the project manager.
2. Haynes Haynesworth, head of circulation.
3. Gun Bangley, director of the computer center and consultant to the library in developing specifications for the hardware and software.
4. Carmen Ghia, lead programmer for Mr. Bangley. Ms. Ghia has been a program analyst for 10 years and has worked often with the library in its automation programs in the past.

THE EVALUATION PROCESS

Several steps were involved in the evaluation process:

Adherence to the Library's Requirements. An evaluation of responses to the RFP indicated that 3 vendors (Handy-Dandy, All-Right Systems, and Solve-All Company) stated they could meet all the library's requirements (see Chart K-1). Upon further examination, discussions with the bidder, and conversations with other users, the team concluded that the ABC Company's system could not meet a large number of requirements.

Comparison of System Hardware. Since 3 vendors indicated they could meet all the library's requirements, some additional comparisons were considered necessary. A comparison of the hardware components was undertaken, with each component weighted on a scale of 1 to 10, depending upon how close it met the library's requirements (see Chart K-2). Three firms—Handy Dandy, All-Right Systems, and Solve-All— compared favorably, with scores of 89, 87, and 86 respectively. Again, the ABC Company's equipment did not seem to meet all the library's requirements.

Cost Comparisons. The bids submitted by the 4 vendors were next evaluated and compared (see Chart K-3). While the ABC Company's bid was lowest, the system offered did not meet the library's minimum requirements specified in the RFP. Also, this system ranked low in the comparison of system hardware. Of the others, the lowest bid was submitted by the Handy Dandy Systems, Inc., whose bid was $27,002 lower than the bid of All-Right Systems, and $78,022 lower than that of Solve-All Company. It should be noted that, while annual operating costs were not considered in the RFP, an earlier preliminary study and comparison of alternative systems showed that the Handy-Dandy System's system's estimated operating costs for 5 years was $35,200 less than that for the Solve-All system. The All-Right system was not studied at that time because the company was organized after that preliminary comparison was made.

Demonstration of Systems. While preliminary results showed that the Handy-Dandy system would be the best and lowest bidder, a demonstration of the system was requested. When the demonstration was conducted, the Handy-Dandy system performed as promised.

RECOMMENDATION OF BEST AND LOWEST BID

Based upon its deliberations, the evaluation team unanimously recommends that the Handy-Dandy system is the best and lowest bidder and should be awarded a contract to supply the automated circulation system for the library. A summary of the factors which led to this conclusion can be found in Chart K-4.

Chart K-1. Summary of a Comparison of Vendor Responses to Requirements in the RFP

REQUIREMENT*	Handy-Dandy	All-Right Systems	Solve-All Company	ABC Company
1. Can operate in a multibranch, multitype situation	Yes	Yes	Yes	Yes
2. Retains all bibliographic records in MARC format	Yes	Yes	Yes	No
3. Interfaces with OCLC (or RLIN or WLN)	Yes	Yes	Yes	No
4. Prints a report of all items which circulate more than a specific number of times	Yes	Yes	Yes	Yes
5. Will allow the library to alter software	Yes	Yes	Yes	No
6. Can deliver by time wanted	Yes	Yes	Yes	Yes
7. Can use a data cassette recorder	Yes	Yes	Yes	Yes
8. Provides circulation statistics online via CRTs	Yes	Yes	Yes	Yes
9. Can be interconnected with other computers	Yes	Yes	Yes	No
10. Protects privacy of all individuals	Yes	Yes	Yes	Yes
11. Has a system of passwords to control or limit access to all files and functions	Yes	Yes	Yes	Partially
12. Allows borrower registration data to be entered online while patron is waiting	Yes	Yes	Yes	Yes

*Sample—Not all requirements are shown.

Chart K-2. Summary of a Comparison of Hardware Components

COMPO-NENT	Handy-Dandy	All-Right Systems	Solve-All Company	ABC Company
Internal storage				
Bid	128KB (10)	128KB (10)	96KB (7)	128KB (10)
Expand-able to	256KB (10)	256KB (10)	96KB (4)	256KB (10)
Operator console Speed	30 cps (10)	180 cps (10)	15 cps (5)	30 cps (10)
Magnetic disk storage				
Bid	192MB (10)	192MB (10)	192MB (10)	96MB (5)
Expand-able to	300MB (10)	300MB (10)	300MB (10)	192MB (5)
Magnetic tape				
Density	1600 BPI (10)	1600 BPI (10)	800 BPI (10)	800 BPI (10)
Speed	20 IPS (9)	15 IPS (7)	25 IPS (10)	15 IPS (7)
Printer				
Print positions	132 (10)	132 (10)	132 (10)	132 (10)
Speed	180 cps (10)	200 cps (10)	200 lpm (10)	60 cps (5)
Total Scores	89 points	87 points	86 points	72 points

Chart K-3. Summary of Costs Bid by Vendors

COST ELEMENT	Handy-Dandy	All-Right Systems	Solve-All Company	ABC Company
Central processing unit	$ 18,500	$ 21,800	$ 17,452	$ 22,150
Operator console	2,000	4,552	1,800	2,500
Magnetic disk storage	52,800	58,450	45,850	28,450
Magnetic tape drive	8,400	10,800	12,400	7,750
Printer	5,000	4,500	820	3,240
Communications control	1,000	800	1,600	500
CRTs	36,000	38,400	20,000	18,500
Scanning wands	20,000	22,000	21,800	20,500
System software	15,000	10,000	8,000	2,000
Application software	18,000	25,000	30,000	15,000
Staff training and manuals	*	1,000	*	5,000
Hardware maintenance for 5 years	160,000	158,000	240,000	155,500
Software maintenance for 5 years	20,000	28,400	35,000	10,000
Totals	$356,700	$383,702	$434,722	$291,090

*Included in application software costs.

Chart K-4. A Summary of Factors upon Which the Recommendation of Best and Lowest Bidder Was Based

DECISION FACTOR	Handy-Dandy	All-Right Systems	Solve-All Company	ABC Company
Vendors state they meet all requirements in the RFP	Yes	Yes	Yes	Yes
Evaluation team determines that vendors meet all requirements	Yes	Yes	Yes	No
Score after a comparison of system software	89	87	86	72 (Does not meet minimum hardware requirements.)
Total costs bid	$356,700	$383,702	$434,722	$291,090

Appendix L
A Sample Set of Specifications for Preparing a Computer Room Site

Following are specifications for renovation of Room B.102 in the Library Building to house the minicomputer system which will support our new circulation system and, eventually, our acquisitions system.

ELECTRICAL POWER

Install the following receptacles in the exact locations indicated on Layout 1.* The numbers below correspond to the numbers on the layout.

1. One Hubbel 9450 or NEMA 14-50R receptacle, single phase, 240 volts, 40 amps, for the central processing unit.
2. Three Hubbel 2513 receptacles for the disk drives, 208 volts, 3-phase, 8 amps per phase in use, maximum surge at start-up: 30 amps/PH for 12 seconds.
3. Ten 5-15R (3-prong) receptacles behind the CPU cabinet, 120 volts, .025 amps.
4. Eight 5-15R (3-prong) receptacles, 120 volts, scattered around the walls, 2 per wall, for miscellaneous use.

There must be a separate circuit for these receptacles from all other electrical power in the building and the circuit must have its own set of circuit breakers.

CABLING

Drill a hole for cabling to the CRTs behind the CPU site, marked on Layout 1.* Use Belden cable # 8723 or its equivalent, shielded-pair

*Layout 1 has not been included with this example.

twisted cable (4 wires), 22-gauge. Leave at least 20 feet of extra cable at each CRT site and at least 15 feet at the CPU site for connecting the equipment. Label the end of each cable, both at the CRT and the CPU sites.

AIR CONDITIONING

Modify the air conditioning supplying the room to maintain the temperature at a constant 70 degrees Fahrenheit and a humidity range of 40 to 60 percent. The following specifications can be used in computing the air conditioning load:

1. The CPU will generate a maximum of 4,100 BTUs per hour.
2. The magnetic tape drive will generate a maximum of 3,400 BTUs per hour.
3. Each of the 3 magnetic disk drives will generate 6,800 BTUs per hour.

Circulation of air is also very important. Heat from the magnetic disk drives, which generate a lot of heat, must be dispersed rapidly from the equipment to avoid the heat buildups which will cause malfunctions and possible damage to the devices. The computer system will be operated 24 hours a day, 7 days a week.

FLOORS

The carpeting in the room must be removed completely and vinyl tile installed. Color samples are attached.

SHELVING

After the new flooring has been installed, the shelving to be supplied by the library must be attached to the wall as indicated in Layout 1.*

FIRE EXTINGUISHER

The 2 fire extinguishers, to be supplied by the library, must be installed at the 2 points indicated in Layout 1.*

DOOR LOCKS

A new lock must be installed on the door to the computer room, and the lock on the supply room door must be repaired.

*Layout 1 has not been included with this example.

Appendix M

Two Sample Job Descriptions for Positions in a Computer-Based Library System

JOB 1

Job Title: Library Assistant II
Department: Bibliographic Control Department
Reports To: Manager of Copy Edit and Input Unit

General Responsibilities

Under supervision of the manager of the Copy Edit and Input Unit, searches the OCLC data base to locate records for materials being cataloged, edits records found to match the materials, locates copy for materials not in the data base, and enters into the OCLC system those records for which copy was located.

Specific Duties

1. Searches the OCLC data base by one or more search keys to locate records for materials being cataloged and edits records found to match the materials in hand (60 percent).

   a. Receives a truck of materials from the Acquisitions Department, with work forms inserted in materials, and initials and dates the truck's work control form.
   b. Determines and enters for each title on the truck the search key(s) necessary to locate its record in the OCLC data base.
   c. Verifies that each OCLC record found matches the title in hand.
   d. Determines and enters changes, if necessary, to make the OCLC record match the title in hand.

e. Copies the LC classification number onto the work form for a title, then signs the forms for later accountability.
f. Commands the system to save the edited record for later revision.
g. Moves material not located in the data base to another truck.
h. When all titles on the truck have been processed, records statistics on the work control form, initials and dates the form, and releases the truck to the reviser.

2. Searches for LC copy for materials not found in the OCLC data base and edits records found (25 percent).

a. Signs and dates the work control form on the truck of materials not located in the OCLC data base.
b. Searches for LC copy for each title.
c. Prepares an OCLC input form for each title.
d. Verifies subject headings for each title.
e. Verifies each class number in the shelf list.
f. Initials each input form for later accountability.
g. Removes material for which no cataloging/classification copy was found to another truck.
h. When all titles on the truck have been processed, records work statistics on the work control form, signs and dates the form, and releases the truck to the reviser.

3. Performs other related duties as required (2 percent).

Supervision

Received: Works under general supervision of a Library Assistant III. All work is revised.
Given: None.

Education/Experience

High school diploma and one year's library experience, or 2 year's of college or equivalent business school training beyond the high school diploma. Experience with OCLC or with an interactive computer system desirable but not mandatory.

Skills

Typing ability required. Keyboarding skills on an interactive computer terminal desirable but not mandatory.

Complexity of Job

Follows detailed instructions and standard, established practices. Some latitude of independent decision making. Errors are usually serious, but easily corrected, except in realm of public contact. Difficult or unusual questions or problems referred to supervisor.

JOB 2

Job Title: Circulation Supervisor, Level III
Department: Circulation Department
Reports To: Manager of Readers Service

Scope

Responsible for the day-to-day operation of the Circulation Department, including coordinating and organizing the activities of the unit and the training and supervision of the full-time staff and student assistants.

Specific Duties

1. Responsible for overseeing all operations in the area, including circulation, reserve, photocopy service, carrel service, traces, and typewriter rental.
2. Responsible for the training of all full-time staff and student assistants.
3. Responsible for the supervision of all full-time staff and student assistants.
4. Assists in the interviewing and hiring of full-time staff and student assistants.
5. Participates in the evaluation of all staff members.
6. Assists in the scheduling of student assistants as hired and at the beginning of each semester.
7. Responsible for coordinating temporary changes in student schedules.
8. Responsible for the scheduling of staff for special hours and interim periods.
9. Works at the circulation and reserve desks.
10. Supervises and assists in the production and mailing of all overdue, fine, and recall notices.
11. Supervises and assists in patron registration and maintenance of the patron data base.
12. Responsible for the carrel service—records, keys, carrel checks, etc.
13. Responsible for the trace service, including seeing that shelves are searched for traced material.
14. Responsible for seeing that the library is opened to the public on regular working days.
15. Operates the computer—brings it up, takes it down, restarts it as necessary, helps with backup as needed, etc.
16. Responsible for all circulation transactions made in the item maintenance function.

17. Responsible for discharging and handling records for all special checkouts returned.
18. Maintains files, records, and statistics.
19. Prepares reports as needed.
20. Conducts routine correspondence.
21. Responsible for the time-worked records for full-time staff and students.
22. Orders supplies and maintains inventory of supplies.
23. Interprets policy and recommends policy changes.
24. Responsible for fire door checks and alarm and light panel checks.
25. Keeps the librarian informed concerning activities within the unit.
26. Serves on night and weekend duty in regular rotation.
27. Performs related duties as required.

Supervision

Received: Works under the supervision of the Reader Services Librarian and the indirect supervision of the Associate Librarian for Public Services. All work is to be performed in accordance with established library policies and procedures.

Given: Reserve Assistant I, Photocopy Assistant I, and from 10 to 15 student assistants.

Education and Experience

Required: Bachelor's degree with one year library experience, or 2 years of college with 2 years of library experience, or high school diploma with 3 years of library experience.

Preferred: College courses in business and/or business school courses. Office, business, supervisory, or related experience.

Skills and Abilities

Required: Typing, filing, good penmanship, ability to produce accurate work, ability to organize work effectively, ability to train and supervise staff, ability to establish and maintain effective working relationships with others and to work well with the public.

Preferred: Typing (40 wpm with 5 or fewer errors per minute).
Filing (alphabetic; 50 cards in 5 minutes with 3 or fewer errors; numeric: 10 cards in 1 minute with no more than 1 error).
Penmanship (to be graded according to educational standards).
Proficiency in operating computer terminals.
Basic math skills.

Appendix N
A Sample General Orientation Guide for a Computer-Based Circulation System

PURPOSE OF THE SYSTEM

The purpose of the circulation system is to provide a means by which patrons can borrow materials from the library's collections and to provide accountability for these loaned materials.

SUBSYSTEMS OF THE SYSTEM

The circulation consists of 6 subsystems or functions: borrower control; charge-renewals; discharges; fines; holds; and overdues and other notices and reports.

Borrower Control Function. The purpose of this subsystem is to provide a means of registering and issuing identification cards to those who wish to borrow materials from the library. In addition, it provides methods of changing or updating information about borrowers and deleting borrowers no longer wanting to use the library. The records of individual borrowers, which include personal information, lists of materials on loan with those overdue or lost tagged, and fines owed, may be viewed and consulted upon demand.

Charge-Renewal Function. This subsystem provides a means by which borrowers may check out library materials for designated periods of time. After a borrower identification number is scanned, the system checks the patron's record to make certain that items are not overdue or fines owed and notifies the operator of any delinquencies so that a decision can be made whether to continue with the transaction. If the loan is made, the system calculates the due date, records the transaction in the circulation file, and prints a date-due slip. A renewal is made by discharging an item, then recharging it to a borrower.

Discharge Function. This subsystem provides a means by which loan transactions are terminated after materials have been returned by borrowers. Fines owed are computed and posted to the borrowers' records. If a hold has been placed on the returned item, the system prompts the operator to put it aside for further processing later.

Fines Function. This subsystem is used when borrowers wish to pay fines or when fines are adjusted or forgiven.

Holds Function. This subsystem provides a means by which patrons can register to borrow items in circulation as soon as they are returned and discharged. If several patrons place a hold on the same item, the system retains the names in the order in which they are placed. A hold may be placed against a specific copy or any copy of a title.

Overdues and Other Notices and Reports. The preparation and printing or display of overdue notices and several other notices and reports are possible in this subsystem. First, second, and third overdues can be prepared for mailing, as well as notices to borrowers that materials they placed on hold are now available, that their registration has expired, and that they owe fines on materials borrowed and returned. The reports which can be prepared and printed or displayed on a terminal include circulation and borrower statistics; lists of borrowers arranged by name, identification number, census tract, or ZIP code; and lists of materials which circulated more than 5 times during a year.

Appendix O
Part of a Sample Procedure Manual for a Computer-Based Circulation System

The borrower control function consists of 2 routines or subfunctions: add a borrower, and display/update/delete a borrower record.

ADD A BORROWER

The purpose of this routine is to enable the staff to enter data about borrowers in the borrower file so that patrons can check out materials on loan. The following procedures should be followed to add a borrower to the file:

1. When the system prompts with PLEASE ENTER FUNCTION, choose option 1 (add a borrower). The system will ask:

BORROWER'S NAME _ _ _ _ _ _ _ _ _ _ _ _ _.

2. Enter the borrower's surname, first name, and any middle initial, using the following format:

JONES, GRIZELDA Q.

   a. The system will search the borrower file for duplication. If there is a match, the system will display the record and ask:

BORROWER ALREADY ON FILE. ENTER NUMBER OF OPTION AT TOP: 1 = ADD THIS NAME. 2 = ADD ANOTHER BORROWER. 3 = STOP.

   The operator then can continue processing or stop.

b. If there is more than one match, the system will display truncated records for each and ask for instructions to continue. In this case, the operator can look at each record one at a time to determine duplication, then either stop the process or proceed to add the new borrower to the borrower file.

If the system finds no duplicate record, it displays the borrower's name on a workscreen.

3. Continue entering the data requested about the borrower being registered.

4. When finished, press the SEND key. The system will check the data entered for validity and for missing information.
   a. If any information is invalid, the system will display:

   ```
   INVALID ENTRY. PLEASE CORRECT THE ERRORS
   INDICATED BELOW.
   ```

   Make the essential corrections and again press the SEND key. The system will repeat the validity check until all information is valid.
   b. If requested information is missing, the system will display:

   ```
   MISSING DATA. PLEASE ENTER THE FOLLOWING:
   ```

   Enter the information as prompted and again press the SEND key. The system will repeat the process until all required information for a borrower has been entered. If all information is valid and complete, the system will file the record in the borrower file and prompt with:

   ```
   BORROWER HAS BEEN ADDED. ENTER NUMBER OF
   OPTION AT TOP: 1 = ADD ANOTHER BORROWER.
   2 = STOP.
   ```

5. Enter the option of your choice.
   a. If you choose to add another borrower, the system will prompt with:

   ```
   BORROWER'S NAME _ _ _ _ _ _ _ _ _ _ _ _ _.
   ```

   In this case, you may repeat steps 2–4 above.

b. If you choose to end the program, the system will display again:

> PLEASE ENTER FUNCTION _ _ _ _ _ _ _.

In this case, you may enter a new function or stop.

DISPLAY/UPDATE/DELETE A BORROWER RECORD

The purpose of this routine is to enable the staff to view a borrower record, change any data for a borrower, or delete the record from the file. The following procedures should be followed:

1. The system will prompt with PLEASE ENTER FUNCTION. Choose option 2 (display/update/delete a borrower record). The system then will ask:

> BORROWER'S NAME _ _ _ _ _ _ _ _ _ _ _ _ _.

2. Enter the borrower's surname, first name, and any middle initial using the following format:

> JONES, GRIZELDA Q.

The system will search the borrower file for matches.
a. If there is no match, the system informs the operator with:

> BORROWER NOT ON FILE. ENTER NUMBER OF OPTION AT TOP: 1 = DISPLAY/UPDATE/DELETE ANOTHER BORROWER. 2 = STOP.

Enter your choice. If you wish to update another record, the system will ask for another borrower's name. If you wish to stop, the system will prompt for another function.
b. If there is more than one match, the system will display numbered, truncated records for each and:

> ENTER LINE # FOR FULL RECORD. U = UPDATE ANOTHER RECORD. NS = NEXT SCREEN. PS = PREVIOUS SCREEN. S = STOP.

Enter your choice. If you wish to update another record, the system will ask for another borrower's name. If you wish to stop, the system will prompt for another function.

c. If only one match is found, the system will display the full record and:

```
ENTER NUMBER OF OPTION AT TOP: 1 = UPDATE REC-
ORD. 2 = DELETE RECORD. 3 = STOP.
```

3. To update a record, choose the UPDATE RECORD option.
   a. Enter the corrected information.
   b. When finished, press the SEND key. The system will check the data for validity and, if information is invalid, will display:

```
INVALID ENTRY. PLEASE REENTER.
```

Make the correction requested and again press the SEND key. The system will repeat the processing until the data are correct.

c. If all updates are valid, the system will file the corrections and prompt with:

```
CORRECTIONS HAVE BEEN MADE. ENTER NUMBER OF
OPTION AT TOP: 1 = UPDATE ANOTHER RECORD.
2 = STOP.
```

Enter your choice. If you wish to continue, the system will return to step 1 and ask for another name. If you wish to stop, the system will ask for another function.

4. To delete a record, choose the delete record option.
   a. If the borrower has outstanding loans or fines, the system will display:

```
BORROWER HAS OUTSTANDING LOANS OR FINES AND
CANNOT BE DELETED. ENTER NUMBER OF OPTION AT
TOP: 1 = DELETE ANOTHER BORROWER. 2 = STOP.
```

Enter your choice. If you wish to delete another borrower, the system will return to step 1 and ask for another borrower's name. If you wish to stop, the system will ask for another function.

b. If your borrower has no outstanding loans or fines, the system
    will delete the record from the borrower file and display:

BORROWER HAS BEEN DELETED. ENTER NUMBER OF
OPTION AT TOP: 1 = DELETE ANOTHER BORROWER.
2 = STOP.

Enter your choice. If you wish to delete another borrower, the
system will return to step 1 and ask for another borrower's
name. If you wish to stop, the system will ask for another
function.

Appendix P
A Sample Guide for a Piece of Hardware: The CRT Terminal

GENERAL

1. Make certain the CAPS LOCK key is down at all times.
2. If you make keying errors, press the "\" for each letter to be corrected, then retype the corrections.
3. Each time an instruction to the computer is entered on the keyboard, the ESCAPE key must be pressed to transmit it.

OPERATING INSTRUCTIONS

1. If the ON/OFF rocker switch is not lit, press the switch until the light is illuminated.
2. Press the BREAK key once firmly to get the computer's attention.
3. When "PW" is displayed on the screen, enter your password while holding down the CTRL key, then press the ESCAPE key.
4. When "PLEASE ENTER FUNCTION" is displayed, enter the first 3 letters of the desired function, then press the ESCAPE key. If the function is unknown, enter a question mark(?), then press the ESCAPE key. A complete list of available functions will be displayed.
5. Follow the prompts given by the computer in using each function.

TROUBLESHOOTING

1. If the screen remains blank and no cursor appears when the CRT is turned on and warmed up:
   a. Check that the CRT power cord is plugged into the electrical outlet.
   b. Check that the CRT actually has been turned on. The red rocker switch on the back of the device should be illuminated. If it is not lit, either the CRT is not receiving power or a fuse has blown.

   c. Check that the brightness control switch on the back of the set has not been turned too far and has blanked out the screen. Rotate the switch until the screen brightens and the cursor appears.

   d. Check that the fuse has not blown.

Note: The CRT takes about one minute to warm up.

2. If the CRT has been turned on and is warmed up, but does not respond to the BREAK key being pressed:

   a. Press the ESCAPE key. The system should respond with "GOODBYE." If it does, press the BREAK key again, and the system should now ask for your password. Continue logging on.

   b. Check that the LINE/LOC key is up. When this key is in the down position, the CRT is disconnected from the computer.

   c. Check that the connector is still attached firmly to the I/O pin connector plug at the back of the CRT. If it is not, reattach it to the I/O (middle) connector plug. If it is loose, push it gently into the plug to make certain it is securely attached.

   d. Check that the HALF/FULL DUPLEX switch on the back of the CRT is set at FULL.

   e. Check that the baud rate switch on the back of the CRT is set at 9600.

Note: There is always the possibility that the computer has stopped running. At this point, if the CRT is not working, call for assistance.

3. If a series of white squares cover the face of the CRT screen after it has been turned on and is warmed up:

   a. Turn the CRT off, using the ON/OFF rocker switch on the back of the device.

   b. Wait 5 seconds.

   c. Turn the CRT on again, using the ON/OFF rocker switch.

The squares should disappear and the cursor should appear. Continue logging in as usual.

4. If numbers appear on the screen when the U, I, O, J, K, and L keys are pressed, check that the NUM key is up. When the NUM key is down, the U, I, O, J, K, and L keys become part of a numeric keyboard similar to that of a 10-key adding machine.

5. If the system stops in the middle of an inquiry or other transaction:

   a. When the system is very busy, some delay in responding to an inquiry or other transaction is normal. This should, however, never be more than a few seconds—never more than a minute.

    b. There is a possibility that you forgot to press the ESCAPE key after entering a request. Press the ESCAPE key at this time and see if the system continues normally.

    c. There is a possibility that you did not follow the prompt instructions on the screen. Usually, the system will reprompt if you err in following its suggestions.

    d. There is a possibility that the computer may have ceased operating.

6. If there are diagonal streaks across the CRT, check that the brightness control switch on the back of the device has not been turned too far. Rotate the switch until the streaks disappear and you achieve an acceptable level of brightness.

Figure P-1. CRT terminal.

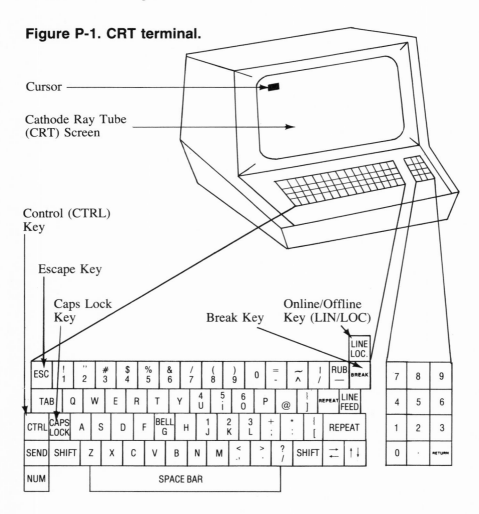

Figure P-2. CRT terminal—back of set.

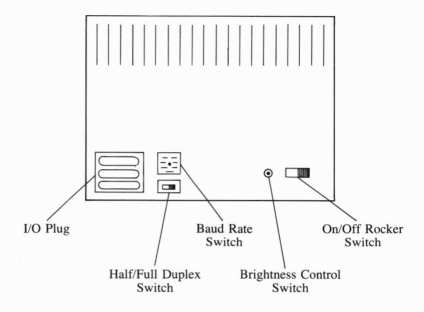

I/O Plug   Baud Rate   On/Off Rocker
                            Switch   Switch

        Half/Full Duplex   Brightness Control
            Switch   Switch

Appendix Q
A Checklist of Special Supplies, Equipment, and Forms for Typical Systems

SPECIAL SUPPLIES AND EQUIPMENT FOR AN IN-HOUSE COMPUTER ROOM

1. Stands or tables for operator's console and printer(s).
2. Shelving for supplies, spare hardware, forms, modems, etc.
3. Magnetic disk pack(s).
4. Magnetic tape on reels or in cassette.
5. Magnetic disk pack storage rack(s).
6. Magnetic tape storage rack(s).
7. Extra ribbons for console and line or serial printer(s).
8. Pressure-sensitive labels for disks and tapes.
9. Fanfold stock paper for printer(s).
10. Lint-free tissues for cleaning equipment.
11. Log book.
12. Antistatic mats.
13. Fire extinguisher(s).
14. Wall clock.
15. Cork bulletin board.
16. Isopropyl alcohol for cleaning equipment.
17. Portable vacuum cleaner.
18. Vacuum cleaner filter bags.
19. Disposable gloves for changing printer ribbons.
20. Racks for operator and procedure manuals.
21. Extra fuses for equipment.
22. Stands or tables for visual display terminal(s).
23. Screwdriver, regular and phillips.
24. Cable bridges.

SPECIAL SUPPLIES AND EQUIPMENT FOR REMOTE TERMINAL STATIONS

1. OCR or bar code labels.
2. Cable bridges.
3. Fuses for OCR or bar code wands and CRTs.
4. Extension cords.
5. Stands or tables for visual display or typewriter terminal(s) and/or slave printer(s).
6. Shelving for modem(s) and other support communications equipment.
7. Extra ribbons for slave printer(s).
8. Fanfold or thermal paper for slave printer(s).
9. Screwdrivers, regular and phillips.

SPECIAL FORMS

1. Order request cards or forms (acquisitions system).
2. Multiple-copy order forms (acquisitions system).
3. Purchase order forms (acquisitions system).
4. Borrower registration cards (circulation system).
5. Borrower identification cards (circulation system).
6. Overdue notice cards, forms, or mailers (circulation system).
7. Recall notice cards, forms, or mailers (circulation system).
8. Hold notice availability cards, forms, or mailers (circulation system).

Glossary

Alphanumeric. Pertaining to a mixture of alphabetic, numeric, and perhaps special characters.

Amp. An amount of electric current measured in units called amperes.

Analyst. Same as *systems analyst*.

Annual Operating Costs. Those costs necessary to maintain and operate a system for a period of one year.

Application Software. One or more computer programs written for a specific library system. Contrast with *system software*.

Arithmetic-Logic Unit. The part of a *central processing unit* in which operations such as adding, subtraction, multiplication, division, and comparison of data are performed.

ASCII. An abbreviation for American Standard Code for Information Interchange, a standardized code for interchange or exchange of data among differing systems. The code consists of a series of 8 bits for each of a defined set of characters.

Automation. See *library automation*.

Auxiliary Equipment. Same as *peripheral equipment*.

Auxiliary or **Secondary Storage.** Storage that supplements the main, primary, or internal storage of a computer system, usually magnetic tape or disk.

Background Program. A low-priority program which can be executed without interfering with higher-priority programs being run at the same time.

Batch Processing. A method of processing data in which a number of records are grouped or batched, then processed together at the same time.

Baud. A method of measuring the rate by which data are transmitted over a communications channel. The speed is roughly equivalent to the number of bits which can be transferred per second.

Binary. Pertaining to the number system with a base of 2. The 2 possibilities are expressed as either 0 or 1.

Bit. An abbreviation of *bi*nary digi*t*, referring to one of the 2 numbers (0 or 1) in the binary number system.

Bits per Inch. The number of bits of data which can be recorded in or along one inch of a recording surface. Usually abbreviated as *BPI*.

Bits per Second. The number of bits of data which can be transmitted over a communications channel in one second. Usually abbreviated as *BPS*.

Block Diagram. A graphic representation of the component subsystems or functions of a system or a subsystem of a system.

BTU. An abbreviation for British thermal unit, a standard unit of heat measurement, equivalent to the amount of heat necessary to raise the temperature of one pound of water by one degree Fahrenheit.

Byte. A group of adjacent binary bits treated as a unit. Usually, 8 bits constitute a byte, which is the equivalent of one character of data.

Cathode Ray Tube Terminal. A terminal device having an electronic vacuum tube on which output from a computer can be displayed. The device usually has a keyboard on which input can be entered. Commonly referred to as a *CRT* or visual display terminal.

Central Processing Unit. The part of a computer system consisting of control, arithmetic-logic, and sometimes primary storage units. Also referred to as the *CPU, main frame,* or *central processor.*

Communications Channel. An electronic or electric link or channel, such as a telephone line or a cable, over which data or information can be transmitted.

Communications Processor. A special device or computer which serves as an interface between another computer and a number of remote devices or terminals.

Compiler. A special computer program which translates instructions written in one language, such as COBOL, FORTRAN, or PL/1, into machine language.

Computer. A machine or device which receives data or information as input, processes the input, and returns the results as output.

Computer-Based Library System. A library system in which some or all of the work is performed by a computer.

Computer Center. An organization responsible for managing, programming, operating, and maintaining one or more computer systems and auxiliary equipment. Synonymous with *data center* or *data processing center.*

Computer Program. A number of instructions which a computer follows in processing data or information.

Computer System. A computing system consisting of a central processing unit, storage units, and input/output devices.

Concentrator. A communications device which allows several low-speed devices to transmit over a single high-speed communications channel.

Control Unit. The part of the central processing unit that receives, interprets, directs, and controls the instructions given the computer to process data.

Corrective Maintenance. Same as *remedial maintenance*.

CPS. Characters per second.

CRT Terminal. See *cathode ray tube terminal*.

Cursor. A special character, usually a dash of light, which may or may not blink, indicating where the next character of data will be displayed on a cathode ray tube terminal.

Data Base. A collection of related files treated as a unit or group. The term is often used synonymously with *file*.

Data Base Management System. A special set of system software which organizes, stores, retrieves, and maintains records in a file or files.

Data Center or **Data Processing Center.** Same as *computer center*.

Data Communication. The process of transmitting and receiving data or information from one point or location to another over a communications channel or link.

Data Element. A predefined unit of data in a record.

Debugging. The process of locating and removing errors in computer programs.

Decision Chart. A chart of data or summary of data on which a decision to accept or reject a system is based.

Decision Flowchart. A special type of flowchart which specifies the operations performed in a system, all decisions which must be made, and alternate courses of action to be taken as a result of the decisions.

Decision Rule. A policy on which to base a judgment as to which of several choices should be selected.

Developmental Costs. The one-time or nonrecurring costs necessary to initialize a system.

Digital Computer. A type of computer which accepts, processes, and stores data in the form of discrete symbols or digits.

Documentation. A collection of documents describing an application, system, subsystem, or subject.

Duplex Channel. A communications channel or link over which data can be transmitted simultaneously in 2 directions; data are transmitted over one channel in one direction, and over another channel in the other direction.

External Storage. Same as *auxiliary storage*.

Feasibility Study. A study undertaken before a system is acquired or implemented to determine if it is practical or will be economical or possible.

File. A collection of related records treated as a unit.

File Conversion. The process of converting data in records of a file to a machine-readable form.

Fixed-Length. Pertaining to fields or parts of records which always contain the same number of characters from record to record.

Flowchart. A graphic or diagrammed representation of a sequence of events or operations performed in a system or subsystem of a system.

Flowchart Symbol. Boxes of various standardized shapes representing operations or processes, decisions, storage, and other activities and pieces of equipment used in constructing flowcharts.

Flowlines. Lines connecting symbols in a flowchart and indicating the direction of flow of work through the system being represented.

Full-Duplex Channel. Same as *duplex channel.*

Functional Subsystem. An independent group of related routines or operations such as charging, discharging, renewals, etc.

Gantt Chart. A project management chart useful to schedule or depict the activities and steps of a project and their times of completion.

Goal. A desired end result of work performed in a system or subsystem of a system.

Half-Duplex Channel. A communications channel or link over which data can be transmitted in both directions, but only in one direction at a time.

Hardware. The physical, mechanical, magnetic, electronic, and electrical components of a computer system.

Hardware Maintenance. Work required to maintain a piece of hardware in good operating condition.

Housekeeping Routines. Tasks vital to the operation of a computer but which do not directly relate to the execution of a library application.

Implementation. The process of carrying out the results of project development and planning.

Information Usage Chart. A chart useful to summarize the data elements found in the various files or records of a system or subsystem of a system.

In-House Computer. A computer physically located in the library and usually dedicated solely to library use.

Input. Data or information entered into a data processing or computer system for processing. Also, the media which contains the data or information.

Input Unit or Device. An electromechanical or electronic device used to enter data or information into a computer system for processing.

Inquiry. A command or request to the computer to locate and present data or information from its storage.

Internal Storage. Same as *primary storage*.

Job Description. A written record of a person's job or position and its requirements.

K. An abbreviation referring to 1,024 bytes of storage.

Large-Scale Computer. The largest size of computer with large primary and auxiliary storage and an ability to handle many applications and users simultaneously.

Layout Chart. A schematic or graphic plan or diagram of the physical space, facilities, and equipment assigned to a system.

Library Automation. The use of an automatic device such as a digital computer to perform some or all operations in a library system.

Library System. See *system*.

Line Controller. A device which manages and monitors the transmission of data over communications channels.

Long-range Plan. A master plan outlining in broad terms the purposes or reasons for automation, any constraints on the efforts, and priorities for development of computer-based systems in the future.

Machine Langage. A language which can be directly accepted or used by a computer.

Machine Readable. In a form which can be sensed or recognized by a computer or other device.

Magnetic Disk. A flat, round metallic disk whose surface is coated with a magnetic recording material on which bits of data can be recorded and thus stored and later retrieved. A number of disks rotating on a central spindle is referred to as a *disk pack*.

Magnetic Tape. A tape coated with a magnetic oxide whose surface can be magnetized with patterns of magnetic bits representing characters of data.

Main Frame. Same as *central processing unit*.

Main Storage. The storage which is an integral part of the central processing unit, used to contain data to be processed and instructions for processing the data during execution of a computer program. Synonymous with *primary storage*.

MARC Format. An acronym for *Ma*chine *R*eadable *C*ataloging. An international standardized format for recording bibliographic information for communication or exchange among libraries and institutions.

Mass Storage. Same as *auxiliary storage*.

Medium-Sized Computer. A computer between the minicomputer and the large-scale computer.

Megabyte. One million bytes of characters of data, usually abbreviated to MB.

Memory. Same as storage, either primary or auxiliary.

Microcomputer. A small, programmable computer usually but not always designed to handle only one application or, at least, a restricted number of applications.

Minicomputer. A small, programmable computer, larger and more versatile than the microcomputer, which can usually handle several applications and users simultaneously.

Mission. The basic reason or purpose why a system or subsystem of a system exists.

Modem. A contraction of *mo*dulator-*dem*odulator. A device which changes or modulates electronic signals to a form which can be transmitted over a communications channel, then back to the original form after transmission. Sometimes referred to as a *data set*.

Modular Approach. A method or technique of separating a system into a number of self-contained parts to facilitate their design, development, or execution. Compare with the *systems approach*.

Network. Two or more libraries organized to share or exchange information and other resources, using established communications links.

Network Chart. A project management chart which can graphically depict the events of a project and their interrelationships.

Network Organization. The staff members who manage and/or operate a network.

Networking. The activity or process of using the services or facilities of a network.

Offline. Equipment or a process not under direct control of a central processing unit of a computer.

Online. Equipment or a process under the direct control of a central processing unit of a computer.

Operating Costs. Same as *annual operating costs*.

Operating System. A special computer program, or set of programs, which manages and controls the execution of other programs. Usually abbreviated to OS.

Operation. A predefined set of steps or tasks established to process input into output in a system or subsystem of a system.

Operator's Console. A special input-output device attached to a computer to enable an operator to control, monitor, and communicate with the system.

Optical Scanner. A device which can sense or read data optically via reflected light and convert it to a machine-readable form.

Output. The end product or results of processing by a data processing or computer system. Also, the medium containing data or information which results from this process.

Output Unit or Device. An electromechanical or electronic device used to present or record data or information resulting from processing by a data processing or computer system.

Peripheral Devices, Units, or **Equipment.** All equipment of a computer system other than the central processing unit. Synonymous with *auxiliary equipment*.

Phase. A very broad or general part of a project.

Port. A channel providing an entrance or exit for the exchange of data or information between a central processing unit and remote, external units or devices such as CRT terminals.

Preventive Maintenance. Maintenance performed on hardware or software to prevent future malfunctions.

Printer. A device which prints output in the form of human-readable characters on paper or forms.

Primary Storage. Same as *main* or *internal storage*.

Private or **Leased Line.** A communications channel furnished to the library for its exclusive use for the duration of a lease.

Problem Statement. A description or definition of one or more problems underlying or causing a need for a project to develop a new or improved system.

Procedure Manual. A step-by-step manual providing instructions how to use, operate, or manage a system.

Program. Same as *computer program*.

Programmer. A person who designs, codes, tests, debugs, and revises the detailed sets of instructions for a computer.

Programming. The process of designing, coding, testing, debugging, and revising computer programs.

Programming Language. The special language in which computer programs are written.

Project Advisory Committee. A special committee established to advise and assist the project manager during the development of a system.

Project Constraint. Limitation or condition placed on a project.

Project Manager. The person officially assigned the responsibility of completing a project successfully. Also referred to as a *project coordinator* or *director*.

Project Objective. A statement of the end results expected of a project or what is to be accomplished during the endeavor.

Project Outline. A list of the phases, activities, and steps or tasks comprising a project.

Project Schedule. A timetable or calendar of the events which must occur in a project to ensure its successful completion.

Prompt. A helpful statement provided by a computer program reminding an operator to provide specific input or to execute a specific task or operation.

Record. A collection of related items or data elements treated as a unit.

Remedial Maintenance. Maintenance performed to correct, on an unscheduled basis, a specific malfunction in a piece of hardware or in software. Synonymous with *corrective maintenance* and *unscheduled maintenance*.

Remote Processing. The use of a computer from a distance, whereby CRT or typewriter terminals in the library are joined via communications links to a computer located a distance away.

Response Time. The lapsed time between entry or submission of a command, query, or data to a computer system and the return of results or a response.

RFP. An abbreviation for *request for proposal*. A document containing requirements or specifications and other information used to solicit price quotations or bids from manufacturers or vendors for hardware, software, and other services. Sometimes referred to as a *request for quotation* or *request for information,* depending upon the intent of the document.

Secondary Storage. Same as *auxiliary storage*.

Simplex Channel. A communications channel or link over which data or information can be transmitted in one direction only.

Site Preparation. The construction or renovation of the physical space in which a computer or system will be located.

Software. In contrast to hardware, the set of computer programs and related documentation for a computer system or for a specific application.

Software Maintenance. Work required to maintain software in good operating condition.

Subsystem. A component part of a system.

System. An organized set of activities, tasks, or operations performed on information, materials, or other physical objects to achieve a specific end result or purpose.

System Analysis. The thorough examination and analysis of all aspects of a system, activities, or techniques to determine the most efficient and effective method of accomplishing what is to be done.

System Analyst. A person who performs the activities of systems analysis.

System Backup or **Recovery.** The duplication of files or provision of procedures in case of system failure or destruction of files and equipment.

System Design. The planning and development of detailed specifications for a system.

System Environment. The physical space in which a system is housed and operated.

System Goals or **Purposes.** The mission or achievements towards which efforts in maintaining and operating a system are directed.

System Lifespan. The number of years a system is expected to last.

System Project. The organized process or endeavor of developing a new or improved system.

System Requirement. A specification of what a system must do or how it must be designed to satisfy needs, wants, or desires of the staff. A mandatory requirement must absolutely be met, while a desirable requirement enhances a system but need not necessarily be met for a system to be acceptable.

System Software. The software necessary to maintain and operate a computer and facilitate the programming, testing, debugging, and running of application software. Examples of system software include operating systems and utility programs.

Systems Approach. A method by which a library is viewed first as a unified whole rather than as segmented and isolated parts. The library is viewed as a number of interacting and interrelated systems or subsystems organized to accomplish a hierarchy of goals and objectives.

Tag. A one or more character label which identifies or specifies a data element or field.

Task. A predefined unit of work to be performed.

Terminal. A point or location in a computer or data communications system where data or information can enter or leave. Usually, a unit or device for transmitting and receiving data to and from a central processing unit.

Total Systems Concept. The complete integration into one system all the major functions or functional subsystems of the library organization.

Transaction. The record of an event or entity in a system or subsystem of a system.

Transaction Fee. A fee incurred or charged each time a transaction event occurs or is completed.

Transmission Control Unit. A device which performs data checking and editing and terminal polling between a computer and a number of remote terminals.

Turnkey System. A system which has been designed and tested by a manufacturer or vendor and, when installed in the library, is ready to be operated merely by "turning the key."

Update. To alter or add to data in a record of a file.

Utility Program. A special general-purpose computer program, usually supplied by the hardware manufacturer, which performs common or often-repeated tasks such as sorting and merging and duplication of files.

Variable-Length Data or **Records.** A data element or record whose length varies from record to record, depending upon the particular information to be recorded.

Visual Display Unit. See *CRT terminal*.

Work Flow. An organized or coordinated movement of activities or work in a desired direction to accomplish a desired goal or objective.

Work Load. The production output, amount, or volume of work to be accomplished in a system or subsystem during a specified period of time.

Work Sampling. The process of selecting a small part of work for inspection or testing, with the purpose of assuming facts about the whole as a result.

Selected Bibliography

Ackoff, R. L. "Towards a System of Systems Concepts," *Management Science* 17 (July 1971): 661–71.

Advances in Librarianship. New York: Academic Press, 1970–to date.

American National Standards Institute. *Standard X3.5 Flowchart Symbols and Their Usage in Information Processing.* New York: ANSI, 1970.

Annual Review of Information Science and Technology. Vols. 1– , 1966– to date (publisher varies).

Arnold, Robert R.; Hill, Harold C.; and Nichols, Aylmer V. *Modern Data Processing.* 3rd ed. Santa Barbara, CA: Wiley, 1978.

Atwood, Jerry W. *The Systems Analyst: How to Design Computer-Based Systems.* Rochelle Park, NJ: Hayden Book Co., 1977.

Auerbach Data World. 4 looseleaf volumes. Pennsauken, NJ: Auerbach Publishers, 1978–to date.

Avram, Henriette D. *MARC: Its History and Implications.* Washington, DC: Library of Congress, 1975.

Barkalow, Pat. "Conversion of Files of Circulation Control," *Journal of Library Automation* 12 (September 1979): 209–13.

Barnes, Ralph M. *Work Sampling.* 2nd ed. New York: Wiley, 1957.

Bellomy, Fred L. "Management Planning for Library Systems Development," *Journal of Library Automation* 2 (December 1969): 187–217.

Bertalanffy, Ludwig Von. *General Systems Theory.* New York: Braziller, 1968.

Bingham, J. E., and Davies, G. W. P. *A Handbook of Systems Analysis.* 2nd ed. New York: Halsted Press, 1978.

Bohl, Marilyn. *Flowcharting Techniques.* Chicago: Science Research Associates, 1971.

Bonn, Jane H., and Heer, Phillip R. "Terminal Equipment for On-Line Interactive Information Retrieval Using Telecommunications," *Special Libraries* 67 (January 1976): 30–39.

Booth, Grayce M. *Functional Analysis of Information Processing: A Structured Approach for Simplifying Systems Design.* New York: Wiley, 1973.

Boss, Richard W. "Circulation Systems: The Options," *Library Technology Reports* 15 (January–February 1979): 7–105.

_____. "General Trends in Implementation of Automated Circulation Systems," *Journal of Library Automation* 12 (September 1979): 198–202.

Brandon, Dick H., and Segelstein, Sidney. *Data Processing Contracts: Structure, Contents and Negotiation.* New York: Van Nostrand-Reinhold, 1976.

Bruer, J. Michael. "The Public Relations Component of Circulation System Implementation," *Journal of Library Automation* 12 (September 1979): 214–18.

Burgess, Thomas K. "A Cost Effectiveness Model for Comparing Various Circulation Systems," *Journal of Library Automation* 6 (June 1973): 75–86.

Burns, Robert W. "A Generalized Methodology for Library Systems Analysis," *College & Research Libraries* 32 (July 1971): 295–303.

Butler, Brett. "State of the Nation in Networking," *Journal of Library Automation* 8 (September 1975): 200–20.

Butler, Brett; Aveney, Brian; and Scholz, William. "The Conversion of Manual Catalogs to Collection Data Bases," *Library Technology Reports* 14 (March–April 1978): 109–206.

Carter, Ruth C. "Systems Analysis as a Prelude to Library Automation," *Library Trends* 21 (April 1973): 505–21.

Chapin, Ned. "Flowcharting with the ANSI Standard: A Tutorial," *Computing Surveys* 2 (June 1970): 119–46.

_____. *Flowcharts.* Philadelphia, PA: Auerbach Publishers, 1971.

Chapman, Edward A.; St. Pierre, Paul L.; and Lubans, John. *Library Systems Analysis Guidelines.* New York: Wiley-Interscience, 1970.

Chapman, Edward A. "Planning for Systems Study and Systems Development," *Library Trends* 21 (April 1973): 470–92.

Churchman, C. West. *The Systems Approach.* New York: Delta Books, 1968.

Cleland, David I., and King, William R. *Systems Analysis and Project Management.* 2nd ed. New York: McGraw-Hill, 1975.

Clinic on Library Applications of Data Processing, University of Illinois. *Proceedings*. Urbana, IL: University of Illinois Graduate School of Library Science, 1963– to date.

Cochran, William G. *Sampling Techniques*. 3rd ed. New York: Wiley, 1977.

Corey, James F., and Bellomy, Fred L. "Determining Requirements for a New System," *Library Trends* 21 (April 1973): 533–52.

Crum, Norman J. "Library Goals and Objectives: Literature Review." ERIC Document ED 082 794.

Daiute, R. J., and Gorman, K. A. *Library Operations Research*. Dobbs Ferry, NY: Oceana Publishers, 1974.

Datapro Research Corporation. *Datapro 70: The EDP Buyer's Bible*. 3 looseleaf volumes. Delran, NJ: Datapro Research Company, 1973– to date.

Dougherty, Richard M., and Heinritz, Fred J. *Scientific Management of Library Operations*. New York: Scarecrow Press, 1966.

Duchesne, Roderick M. "Analysis of Costs and Performance," *Library Trends* 21 (April 1973): 587–604.

Encyclopedia of Computer Science and Technology. Vols. 1–14. New York: Dekker, 1975–80.

Encyclopedia of Library and Information Science. Edited by Allen Kent and Harold Lancour. New York: Dekker, 1969–to date.

Fasana, Paul J. "Systems Analysis," *Library Trends* 21 (April 1973): 465–78.

Fient, Hans G. "Management of the Acquisition Process for Software Products," *Management Information* 2 (1973): 153–64.

FitzGerald John M., and FitzGerald, Ardra F. *Fundamentals of Systems Analysis*. New York: Wiley, 1973.

Gardner, Jeffrey J., and Webster, Duane E. *The Formulation and Use of Goals and Objectives Statements in Academic and Research Libraries*. Washington, DC: Association of Research Libraries, Office of University Library Management Studies, 1974.

Goodell, John S. *Libraries and Work Sampling*. Edited by Robert E. Kemper. Littleton, CO: Libraries Unlimited, 1975.

Gough, Chet, and Srikantaiah, Taverekere. *Systems Analysis in Libraries: A Question and Answer Approach*. Hamden, CT: Linnet Books, 1978.

Griffin, Hillis L. "Implementing the New System: Conversion, Training, and Scheduling," *Library Trends* 21 (April 1973): 565–74.

Hartman, W.; Matthes, H.; and Proeme, A. *Management Information Systems Handbook: Analysis, Requirements Determination, Design and Development, Implementation and Evaluation.* New York: McGraw-Hill, 1968.

Hayes, Robert M., and Becker, Joseph. *Handbook of Data Processing for Libraries.* 2nd ed. Los Angeles: Melville Publishing Company, 1974.

Heiliger, Edward M., and Henderson, Paul B. *Library Automation: Experience, Methodology and Technology of the Library as an Information System.* New York: McGraw-Hill, 1971.

Heinritz, Fred J. "Analysis and Evaluation of Current Library Procedures," *Library Trends* 21 (April 1973): 522–32.

Hice, G. F.; Turner, W. S.; and Cashwell, L. F. *System Development Methodology.* Rev. ed. Amsterdam: North-Holland Publishing Company, 1978.

Jacob, Mary Ellen L. "Standardized Costs for Automated Library Systems," *Journal of Library Automation* 3 (September 1970): 207–17.

Juergens, Bonnie. "Staff Training Aspects of Circulation System Implementation," *Journal of Library Automation* 12 (September 1979): 203–8.

Kaplan, Louis, ed. *Reader in Library Services and the Computer.* Washington, DC: NCR Microcard Editions, 1971.

Kilgour, Frederick G. "Computer-Based Systems, a New Dimension to Library Cooperation," *College & Research Libraries* 34 (March 1973): 137–43.

Kindred, Alton R. *Data Systems and Management: An Introduction to Systems Analysis and Design.* Englewood Cliffs, NJ: Prentice-Hall, 1973.

Knox, F. M. *The Knox Standard Guide to the Design and Control of Business Forms.* New York: McGraw-Hill, 1965.

Kountz, J. C. "Library Cost Analysis: A Recipe," *Library Journal* 97 (February 1, 1972): 459–64.

Lazzaro, Victor, ed. *Systems and Procedures: A Handbook for Business and Industry.* 2nd ed. Englewood Cliffs, NJ: Prentice-Hall, 1968.

"The Library and the Computer Center," *Journal of Library Automation* 12 (December 1979): 362–78.

Library Automation: The State of the Art II. Edited by Susan K. Martin and Brett Butler. Chicago: American Library Association, 1975.

Lockwood, J. D. "Involving Consultants in Library Change," *College & Research Libraries* 38 (November 1977): 498–508.

Lubans, John R., and Chapman, Edward A. *Reader in Library Systems Analysis*. Washington, DC: NCR Microcards, 1975.

McInerney, Thomas F., and Vallee, Andre J. *A Student's Guide to Flowcharting*. Englewood Cliffs, NJ: Prentice-Hall, 1973.

MacKenzie, A. Graham. "Systems Analysis as a Decision-Making Tool for the Library Manager," *Library Trends* 21 (April 1973): 493–504.

Martin, James. *Introduction to Teleprocessing*. Englewood Cliffs, NJ: Prentice-Hall, 1972.

Martin, Susan K. "Turnkey Systems: How to Avoid Locking Yourself In," *American Libraries* 10 (February 1979): 89–91.

Mathews, William D. "Advances in Electronic Technologies," *Journal of Library Automation* 11 (December 1978): 299–307.

Matthews, Joseph R. "The Four Online Bibliographic Utilities: A Comparison," *Library Technology Reports* 15 (November–December 1979): 665–838.

Maynard, H. B., ed. *Industrial Engineering Handbook*. 3rd ed. New York: McGraw-Hill, 1971.

Meadow, Charles T. *The Analysis of Information Systems*. 2nd ed. Englewood Cliffs, NJ: Prentice-Hall, 1973.

Minder, Thomas. "Application of Systems Analysis in Designing a New System," *Library Trends* 21 (April 1973): 553–64.

Mitchell, Betty Jo; Tanis, Norman E.; and Jaffe, Jack. *Cost Analysis of Library Functions: A Total System Approach*. Greenwich, CT: JAI Press, 1978.

Moder, Joseph, and Phillips, Cecil R. *Project Management with CPM and PERT*. 2nd ed. New York: Van Nostrand-Reinhold, 1970.

Nadler, Gerald. *Work Design: A Systems Concept*. Rev. ed. New York: Irwin, 1970.

On-Line Revolution in Libraries: Proceedings of the 1977 Conference in Pittsburgh, Pennsylvania. Edited by Allen Kent and Thomas J. Galvin. New York: Dekker, 1978.

Optner, Stanford L. *Systems Analysis for Business Management*. 3rd ed. Englewood Cliffs, NJ: Prentice-Hall, 1975.

Palmer, Richard Phillips. *Case Studies in Library Computer Systems*. New York: R. R. Bowker, 1973.

Patrinostro, Frank S. *A Survey of Commonplace Problems in Library Automation*. Peoria, IL: LARC, 1973.

Price, Douglas S. "Rational Cost Information: Necessary and Obtainable," *Special Libraries* 65 (February 1974): 49–57.

Raffel, Jeffrey A., and Shisko, Robert. *Systematic Analysis of University Libraries: An Application of Cost-Benefit Analysis of the M.I.T. Libraries*. Cambridge, MA: MIT Press, 1969.

Reader in Operations Research for Libraries. Edited by Peter Brophy, Michael K. Buckland, and Anthony Hindle. Englewood, CO: Information Handling Services, 1976.

Ross, J., and Brooks, J. "Costing Manual and Computerized Library Circulation Systems," *Program* 6 (1972): 217–27.

Salmon, Stephen R. *Library Automation Systems*. New York: Dekker, 1975.

Salton, Gerard. *Dynamic Information and Library Processing*. Englewood Cliffs, NJ: Prentice-Hall, 1975.

Sanders, Donald H. *Computers in Society*. 2nd ed. New York: McGraw-Hill, 1977.

Scholz, William H. "Computer-Based Circulation Systems—A Current Review and Evaluation," *Library Technology Reports* 13 (May 1977): 231–325.

Sippl, Charles J., and Sippl, Charles P. *Computer Dictionary*. Indianapolis, IN: Sams, 1974.

Smith, G. C. K., and Schofield, J. L. "Administrative Effectiveness: Times and Costs of Library Operations," *Journal of Librarianship* 3 (October 1971): 245–66.

Spencer, Donald D. *The Illustrated Computer Dictionary*. Columbus, OH: Charles E. Merrill, 1980.

Swihart, Stanley J., and Hefley, Beryl F. *Computer Systems in the Library*. Los Angeles: Melville Publishing Company, 1973.

Szweda, Ralph A. *Information Processing Management*. 2nd ed. New York: Van Nostrand-Reinhold, 1978.

Thomas, P. A. *Task Analysis of Library Operations*. London: Aslib, 1971.

"Understanding the Utilities: An Introduction to the Birth and Development of the Major Online Bibliographic Utilities," *American Libraries* 11 (May 1980): 262–79.

Van Tassel, Dennis. *Computer Security Management*. Englewood Cliffs, NJ: Prentice-Hall, 1972.

Vardaman, Patricia B. *Forms for Better Communication*. New York: Van Nostrand-Reinhold, 1971.

Veaner, Allen B. "Major Decision Points in Library Automation," *College & Research Libraries* 31 (September 1970): 299–312.

Warheit, I. A. "The Automation of Libraries: Some Economic Considerations," *Special Libraries* 63 (January 1972): 1–7.

————. "Design of Library Systems for Implementation with Interactive Computers," *Journal of Library Automation* 3 (March 1970): 65–78.

————. "When Some Library Systems Fail—Is It the System or the Librarian?" *Wilson Library Bulletin* 46 (September 1971): 52–58.

Wiest, Jerome D., and Levy, Ferdinand K. *A Management Guide to PERT/CPM, with GERT/PDM/DCPM and Other Networks.* 2nd ed. Englewood Cliffs, NJ: Prentice-Hall, 1977.

Willoughby, Theodore C., and Senn, James. *Business Systems.* Cleveland, OH: Association for Systems Management, 1975.

Young, Arthur P. "Generating Library Goals and Objectives," *Illinois Libraries* 56 (November 1974): 862–66.

Index

Compiled by Linda Schexnaydre